The
Health Care Executive's
Job Search

Tyler's Guide to Success

AMERICAN COLLEGE OF HEALTHCARE EXECUTIVES MANAGEMENT SERIES

Anthony R. Kovner, Series Editor

The
Health Care Executive's
Job Search

Tyler's Guide to Success

J. Larry Tyler

Health Administration Press
Chicago, IL 1996

98   97   96   5   4   3   2

Library of Congress Cataloging-in-Publication Data

Tyler, J. Larry
  The health care executive's job search : Tyler's guide to success /
J. Larry Tyler.
     p.   cm.
  Includes bibliographical references and index.
  ISBN 1-56793-013-1
  1. Health services administrators—Vocational guidance. 2. Job hunt-ing. I. Title.
RA971.T95   1994   650.4'02461—dc20   94-6173 CIP

The paper used in this publication meets the minimum requirements of American National Standard for Information Sciences—Permanence of Paper for Printed Library Materials, ANSI Z39.48-1984.

Health Administration Press
A division of the Foundation of the
  American College of Healthcare Executives
1021 East Huron Street
Ann Arbor, Michigan 48104-9990
(313) 764-1380

To my parents, Marjorie and James Tyler

Contents

Foreword

Larry Tyler's new book offers you an invitation to have an in-depth conversation with one of our nation's foremost executive search consultants. In the brief preface, you are candidly informed about the audience this book was written for, and about what is to follow. This book is, in every sense of the word, a "how to" book for those individuals in the health care field who are planning a job change within that industry. As you read, you will share in not only the experiences of Larry Tyler over a 15-year period, but also the experiences of Tyler & Company's professional staff.

Chapter 1 thrusts you into the first necessary step in your job search, writing a historical resume. You are warned early on that this is only the first step, not the most important one. This chapter sets the practical and straightforward tone for the following thirteen chapters. The chapter on resume preparation ends with a checklist that you would do well to follow scrupulously. Four appendixes follow this chapter: examples of an excellent historical resume, a historical resume with incorrect use of dates, a functional resume, and a narrative resume. If you follow the practical advice in this chapter, you most assuredly do not need to engage a resume firm or consultant to assist you in your resume preparation.

In the first paragraph of Chapter 2 (cover letters), the author's straightforward style comes through in spades: Cover letters are the most basic part of the job search process. . . . Avoid gimmicks. Keep in mind that the cover letter complements your resume; they work hand-in-hand to present you and your career goals in the most professional light." The six appendixes that follow give you both positive and negative examples of cover letters.

Your reference list "is the third part of the job search trilogy." Chapter 3 is the most helpful and practical discussion of developing a reference list that I have ever encountered in my three years of graduate studies in human resources, thirty-eight years as a health care executive, and thirteen years as an educator. Mistakes in preparing your reference list can be fatal to your career, so proceed with great care and caution. Read and reread this chapter before contacting your first potential reference. Most well-managed organizations check references by telephone before extending an offer. If they have engaged a professional executive search firm, the search consultant will check the references by telephone. You are warned in the chapter of the potential dangers if you have not had a candid conversation with each individual on your reference list. Those conversations should give you a strong feeling as to whether or not the individual will give you an enthusiastic reference.

At the beginning of Chapter 4, Stephen Rosen is quoted: "Network or not work." This is sound advice for any job applicant and, unfortunately, is vastly misunderstood by most early and mid-career executives. Take seriously the Tyler Networking Technique, and keep your network current and informed about your present position and accomplishments. If you wait until you are ready to begin a job search to start networking, or to update your network, you have waited too long and unnecessarily handicapped your job search.

Chapters 5 and 6 discuss in detail outplacement and recruiting firms. They include updated lists of firms with their current addresses, a most valuable reference source.

Chapter 7 covers the interview, the most important part of the job search. "Individuals can be, and occasionally are, hired without resumes, without cover letters, without reference checks, and even without search firms, but never without an interview. . . . Preparation is essential for you as a candidate if you expect to come out ahead of other candidates who may match you in experience and ability."

A list of places to seek information about the organization and the hiring manager is provided. Do not overlook the value of activating your network to gain accurate candid information.

The "Guidelines to Frequently Asked Interview Questions" is a rich resource for preparing yourself mentally for the interview. The staff of Tyler & Company has also prepared a "Structured Interview Format," a list of questions they usually ask of candidates, included for you as Appendix 7.1. Both lists should be studied and your responses should be carefully considered. You do not want to be caught off-guard or surprised during the interview.

Chapter 7 then discusses thank-you notes (including an example) and the importance of having your own list of questions for the second interview. This is your opportunity to clarify any confusion or doubts you may have from the first round of interviews. Areas of major interest for you are "benefits, the reporting structure and scope of authority, real estate issues, and spousal issues." Since the second interview usually includes your spouse, you should request "the itinerary for the visit, in advance, with the names, titles, and employers of the people with whom you will be meeting." Be sure to "find out about the social events ahead of time and the appropriate dress." This way you and your spouse can be prepared.

Chapter 8 will help you evaluate job offers, assisting you in examining money, opportunity, location, and opportunities for your spouse. Additional factors are included in a checklist. Since employment contracts are today a part of the hiring process, you will want to study carefully Appendix 8.1, "Recommended Employment Contract for Hospital Chief Executive Officers." It contains a great deal that is applicable to any senior management position.

Chapter 9, "Starting Off on the Right Foot," and Chapter 10, "Making the Transition from the Military" are brief chapters but contain practical advice worthy of your study.

In Chapters 11 and 12, questions about gender and racial discrimination, which will be considered by many individuals as "uncomfortable," are raised and discussed in detail. I recommend the interviews with successful women and minorities in health care organizations for reading and thoughtful study by all health care supervisors. These interviews include discussions of career path and personal outlook, stereotypes, biggest hurdle, advice to "up and comers," breaking through the glass ceiling, handling the "solo" and "token" roles, fairness in hiring, and overt vs. unspoken barriers. Chapter 13 follows up with suggestions for strategies to address discrimination in the job search process.

This excellent handbook's final two chapters discuss sources of support and getting motivated for the job search.

You are in for a treat! In addition to offering practical advice, preparing you for each step of the job search process, and making available valuable information, Larry Tyler writes in a conversational mode and includes much humor. This book offers you a highly

valuable consultation with one of our nation's most experienced and
knowledgeable health care search consultants.

                              L. R. (Rush) Jordan
                              Professor, Health Services Administration
                              University of Alabama at Birmingham
                                        and
                              President Emeritus
                              Miami Valley Hospital
                              Dayton, Ohio

Preface

Success is when preparation meets opportunity.

For 18 years I have headed a nationally recognized firm that conducts executive searches for health care organizations. I am therefore in a unique position to offer some practical guidelines to people who are about to undertake a job search in the present competitive job market. What follows is a combination of job-seeking methods (including the Tyler Networking Technique), reference guides, examples of professional correspondence, and anecdotal advice for someone who wants to know how hiring decisions are made in health care.

For some time, I wanted to write a book about the job change process. Not that there aren't already plenty of books on the market that address this subject from almost every aspect imaginable. However, as I consulted with candidates about how to change jobs and started reading the available books to find out which ones to recommend to people, I was disappointed and occasionally appalled at the information thrust upon unsuspecting job seekers. I promised myself that I would eventually write this book with the hope that I could make a difference in someone's life by helping that person through a successful job change. As this book enters its second printing, it is gratifying to know that it is helping more than a few people.

This is a "how to" book. It is a book about how to conduct a successful job search. It will not help you find the meaning of life, and it will not help you examine and redirect your career. This book is aimed at people who already know where they are going—to a more challenging and responsible position in health care—and just need a map showing how to reach that destination. If you are unsure about the kind of job you want or where your career is headed, you need to read other books or get vocational counseling before you start this book.

This book is based upon interviews conducted over a span of 18 years with approximately 1,800 job seekers in the health care field. I owe most of what I know about health care and job change to this group of individuals whom I have had the privilege to get to know. I wish to thank them for sharing their stories with me. It is only through their shared collection of experiences that I have been able to write this book.

This book cannot work miracles or magically place you in a job. Hopefully, it will inspire, amuse, and inform you. But the most vital part is you. You must take responsibility for your own job search. Reading this book is a good first step on your job search journey.

If you can follow the suggestions, tailor them to your own situation, use the available reference materials, and follow through on every step you take, your success is guaranteed. It may take longer than you would like, but you will win. You will get the job you want.

When you finish the book, drop me a line and tell me what you liked or didn't like, and what worked for you. I would appreciate hearing from you.

Acknowledgments

Writing this book has been an endeavor that could only be character-ized as a grueling labor of love. Without the help and encouragement of many individuals, I could not have completed it.

I wish to thank all of the candidates I have ever interviewed who, in detailing their stories, gave me the information about what works and doesn't work when looking for a job. I also want to thank the individuals profiled in Chapters 11 and 12 for letting us tell their stories in order to give inspiration to others. Their willingness to reveal their thoughts is greatly appreciated.

I wish to thank the staff at Health Administration Press for their patience in dealing with a consultant who travels and has lots of other things to do besides writing a book; their persistence is appreciated.

Finally, I wish to thank Judith Curlee, my researcher. Without her help, this book could never have been finalized. Her patient attitude, attention to detail, and sense of humor moved this project along. She has given me a new impression of those who study 16th-century literature, which she hopes to make her life's work.

Part I

The Job Search Trilogy

1

Resumes

A journey of a thousand miles must begin with a single step.

—Lao-Tzu

Warning! A resume is merely a facilitation tool; it is a first step, not an end in itself. Some job seekers believe that the preparation of a good resume is the most important part of their job search, but even the most stellar and professional resume does not ensure success. In truth, a good interview is the most important, so if you only intend to read one chapter in this book, this is not the one. Nonetheless, as you embark on your job search, you will frequently be asked for your resume. Without it, you cannot go to the next step, an interview. Therefore, your job search must begin with the preparation of a resume.

The Three Types of Resumes

There are three types of resumes—historical, functional, and narrative. Because the historical resume is by far and away the most commonly used format, it is the primary focus of this chapter. At the end of the chapter, I will also provide examples of functional and narrative resumes and discuss their appropriate use.

Historical Resumes

A historical resume is arranged in reverse chronological order. Using Appendix 1.1 as an example, let us examine each of the seven individual items in the historical resume in the order they normally appear in:

1. Name, address, and home and business phone numbers
2. Education
3. Experience—responsibilities and accomplishments
4. Professional affiliations
5. Personal information (optional)
6. Outside interests
7. References

Name, Address, and Phone Numbers

Obviously, your name and address are extremely important items to include on your resume. I have actually received resumes that omitted this fundamental information—perhaps in an attempt to create suspense in the reader or on the assumption that the reader has the cover letter at hand. Avoid such poor judgment and tell potential employers your name. Begin each new page with your name in case the pages become separated during review.

Unlike the other items, you do not need to give a heading to this item, but simply use the same highlighting technique used to mark the other six items. In our sample, the candidate has used boldface and uppercase letters to emphasize each separate section. Note also the judicious use of underlining to further focus the reader's attention.

If you have a nickname by which you are better known, you may wish to place it in parentheses after your given name. Also, if you have a doctoral degree, professional certification, or a distinguished fellowship, by all means, place the appropriate initials (for example, CPA, Ph.D., or FACHE) after your name. However, if you have an M.B.A. or B.S., save that information for the education section of your resume.

Always place your home address on the resume, unless you are working out of your office in an outplacement situation—a rare occurrence. Generally, you would not want information related to your job search arriving at your office. However, since most contacts with candidates are made over the telephone at their place of business during normal working hours, it is very important for people to be able to reach you during business hours. If you are concerned about the confidentiality of your own search within your office, include the phrase "(to be used with discretion)" immediately below the business phone number. In addition, include your residence phone number. Be sure to use an answering service or have an answering machine to take your calls at home. The job search process is so difficult that you cannot risk being unavailable to someone who is trying to reach you.

Personal Information

Your resume can contain some personal information, if it is brief. In the sample resume of the hypothetical Richard J. Overachiever, the candidate has chosen not to include any personal information. An employer cannot legally discriminate against an individual on the basis of age, race, sex, color, national origin, or marital status. However, if you are married, you might want to go ahead and mention it, if you believe it will help convey a sense of stability. If you have children, give the number, but not their names or ages. Once I received a resume that not only gave the name and age of the applicant's child, but also little Johnny's most recent accomplishment—potty training. That resume is a prize exhibit in my informal "Ripley's Believe It or Not of Resumes"—a collection of negative examples I have gathered over the years. Don't let your resume become part of my collection!

Job Objectives

Your resume should not include a job objective. Job objectives are either so broad as to be meaningless, or so narrow as to keep you out of the running for a position that you might like to explore. Look at these four job objectives commonly seen on resumes. What do you think that they tell us?

- A meaningful position in hospital administration that allows me to exhibit my skills in strategic planning and marketing
- A position as chief nursing officer in a hospital
- A growth position in a managed care company
- An executive position in a health care environment

Leave the job objective off your resume. Include the job objective in the cover letter you draft to accompany your resume. The cover letter, which I discuss in the following chapter, allows you to tailor your stock resume to the specific job at hand. If you follow my advice and announce your objective in your cover letter, then placing an objective on your resume becomes redundant. Space is at a premium in a first-rate resume.

Education

The next item on the resume, in most cases, is "education." Someone in senior-level management might place this section at the end of the resume, depending upon the individual's professional level. Because a historical resume chronicles your life in reverse order, begin with the highest degree earned; do not indicate the dates that school was attended, only the year in which the degree was conferred. If you have not yet completed your degree, however, show the dates attended and perhaps how far along you are. If you have no intentions of completing your degree, you can say something such as "studies in economics." If you have earned your CPA or passed the bar exam, note this fact in the educational section of your resume. Fellowships, such those sponsored by the American College of Healthcare Executives (FACHE) or the Healthcare Financial Management Association (FHFMA), are usually indicated by placing the initials after your name and describing the fellowship in the "other" section of your resume. If you graduated with honors, include this information in the description of the degree. If you graduated with an M.H.A. and completed a residency, note the location of the residency in the work experience section of the resume. Omit your grade point average.

Experience

Now we reach the most important section of the resume—"experience." Here you describe the jobs that you have held. Two errors are often made by many candidates in this section. The first common error is failing to describe specific responsibilities and accomplishments. Responsibilities and accomplishments are both im-portant, so you should include them in your description of each job. Responsibilities tell the reader about the scope and breadth of the job. Examples of responsibilities you want to note include the number of FTEs supervised, the number of departments reporting to you, the total amount of the budget, and the names of committees on which you served. Accomplishments, on the other hand, demonstrate the scope and breadth of your abilities. Try to offer accomplishments more meaningful than "manning," and "coordinating," and "orchestrating." One concrete way to do so is by quantifying your accomplishments:

- Established a purchasing program that saved $50 million in the first three years
- Reduced accounts receivable from 95 to 75 days
- Processed successful CONs for $5 million in equipment
- Reduced FTEs from 5.4 to 4.5 per adjusted occupied bed

Specificity allows the reader of your resume to understand your impact upon the organization.

The second most common mistake is failing to clearly format employment history within a single organization. Indicate the dates of continuous employment with one organization on the left side and note the dates corresponding to each position within the organization immediately after the job description. If you refer to Appendix 1.1, you see that Richard J. Overachiever has been with Methodist Health Management since 1978, during which time he has held two different jobs. Listing the dates of different positions within one organization separately on the left-hand side of the resume confuses the reader. Appendix 1.2 shows you this mistake: If Richard places both sets of dates over on the left side, he gives the impression that he had two different employers within this one period, when really he moved up within the organization.

To save space and the reviewer's time, try to abbreviate the responsibilities and accomplishments for earlier positions. The further you go back in time, the more important it is to condense your responsibilities and accomplishments. The general rule: Condense heavily the descriptions of jobs held prior to the 10-year mark. People simply do not place as much emphasis on those responsibilities and accomplishments as they do on your current ones. Focus on the truly exceptional projects and tasks you have successfully handled.

Professional Affiliations

The next section, "professional affiliations," rounds out your resume's description of you. Professional affiliations demonstrate your active involvement in the health care profession. Do not, however, overload this section; proliferation of professional affiliations may cause the reader to conclude that the candidate spends more time attending meetings and dealing with outside entities than he or she does at work. The goal of this section is to show that you are active professionally, without causing the reader to question your credibility or your priorities.

First, list the national organizations, designating those in which you are a fellow or in which you have held a leadership position. Then, list any local community and civic organizations in which you participate, particularly if you are a hospital CEO. Be sure to indicate the leadership positions you have held.

Outside Interests

As a complement to your education, work experience, and professional affiliations, the next section, "outside interests," gives the reviewer additional information about your personality. I recommend listing active sports as outside interests. Hospital administrators and health care professionals commonly golf, fish, or play tennis recreationally; by listing these hobbies you provide an opportunity for breaking the ice during your interview. Also, active hobbies, such as sports, will be looked at more favorably than passive hobbies, such as reading or watching films. You should be careful if your outside interests might be considered outside the norm; you can't predict how a reviewer will react to them. For example, say a candidate indicates that he or she is a lepidopterist. How would a reader react to this information? I would predict that most people would not know what "lepidopterist" means, and upon being told that it refers to butterfly collecting, they would look at the candidate askance. Therefore, refrain from listing really offbeat outside interests. Also omit mentioning membership in organizations whose agendas are primarily religious or political.

References

The final section, "references," requires little space on your resume. Although you do want to line up your references in advance, by simply stating on your resume "References furnished upon request," you indicate that you are prepared to provide them. Your actual list of references should be supplied only after the potential employer asks for it, so do not submit the reference list with your resume but have it ready and current for the reviewer's request. Chapter 3 gives further instructions on how to choose references, how to compose the reference list, and how to check your own references.

Why, if you expend all the time and trouble to establish a strong reference list, do I discourage you from submitting the reference list with your resume? First, being a reference can be a time-consuming inconvenience. You don't want potential employers to call your references unless you have a strong and serious interest in the job. Second, if you have supplied the person's name on your resume, some potential employers will ignore protocol and call the reference before ever contacting you. The procedure as I outline it allows you to exercise some control.

The resume and the reference list alike should be printed on good-quality paper. Ideally, you should print your cover letter, resume, and reference list on the same kind of paper, using the same typeface. Use white, ivory, or light beige paper, although recently beige has fallen somewhat out of favor.

Warnings and Reminders for Resume Writing

Danger! Using a home computer to prepare your resume, an increasingly common practice, can be hazardous to your job search. First, because of all the storage space they have, many computer buffs throw everything, including the kitchen sink, into the resume. Remember, your resume should not exceed three pages. The second danger of using your home computer to prepare your resume is the temptation to print it out on your dot matrix printer. Certainly, you can maintain your resume on your home computer, but print it out on the office laser printer or use a professional printer for the final copies.

Do not use gimmicks or attention grabbers to make your resume stand out. The only attention such misguided attempts receive is negative attention. Our in-house "Ripley's Believe It or Not of Resumes" includes resumes printed on pink paper, precrumpled ("don't throw this away without reading it") resumes, and resumes with dollar bills attached (indicating a willingness to invest in a search). My firm has received elaborate brochures and resumes accompanied by hospital promotional material a half-inch thick.

None of these gimmicks benefits the candidate, because what matters is the information we need in order to assess whether the client's job and the candidate's background are a good match. Do not resort to gimmicks to gain attention. Do strive to make your resume the most professional one that the reviewer will see. Highlight the important information, quantify it, and let the process take its course.

You have prepared an accurate and informative resume and are ready to forward it to the reviewer. What next? Proofread your resume. Ask two other people whose intelligence you respect to proofread it for you. Check the correct spelling of any word you are not sure of. Often, someone who receives a resume containing a misspelled word will circle the word and circulate the resume throughout the office for the enjoyment of all. When Marilyn Quayle sent out 5,000 Christmas cards in 1989 with a misspelled word, "beakon," the vice president's wife received national negative publicity, and of course I don't need to mention what her husband's creative spelling, "potatoe" did for him. Don't let that happen to you.

Functional and Narrative Resumes

Although the historical resume is the most useful and common form, I will briefly describe the other two kinds of resumes: functional and narrative resumes. The functional resume groups your different duties, responsibilities, and accomplishments without regard to their historical perspective. Appendix 1.3 is an example of a functional resume. People changing industries might decide to use this format to show how their responsibilities and accomplishments relate to the job in question. Despite what resume houses tell you, functional resumes are very infrequently used. Fewer than 2 percent of resumes received at Tyler & Company are functional resumes. When a candidate with whom we want to work submits a functional resume, we return it and request a historical one.

The other kind of resume is the narrative resume, seen in Appendix 1.4. A narrative resume reads like a letter. Usually, the candidate will highlight the different experiences that pertain to the position for which he or she wants to be considered. As with functional resumes, we ask job seekers to replace a narrative resume with a historical one.

There are a couple of simple reasons why the historical resume is the best format. First, it is easier for the reader to discern the person's employment history and most recent accomplishments. Second, because the most important items are listed on the left, and because we read from left to right, this format is easier to read.

Resume Checklist

- Use the historical format.
- Do not include the job objective.
- Avoid gimmicks.
- Do not exceed three pages.
- Proofread twice.
- Print the resume on high-quality paper.
- Print with a laser printer or a professional print shop.
- Do not submit a photocopy of your resume. Take the time to send an original.

Frequently Asked Questions About Writing a Resume

Question: I am very concerned about the confidentiality of my job search. A friend of mine is willing to act as a middleman on my behalf. Is this a good ploy?

Answer: Absolutely not. Prospective employers do not want to deal with intermediaries in order to contact the individuals, unless the third party is a bona fide employment specialist. Using a buddy as your front person makes you seem incompetent or secretive.

Question: I am interested in three different types of positions and wonder if I should prepare a different resume for each type of job. What is your opinion?

Answer: Not a good idea. You ought to be able to use one resume for every type of job because you can use your cover letter to highlight the experience and training that relates to the position in question.

Question: But what if I am asked to bring a copy of my resume with me to the interview?

Answer: That's fine, but you can still attach a cover letter to the resume to describe your suitability for the job.

Question: I have separated from my employer, but have twelve months in severance pay. What is the best way to show this on my resume?

Answer: After a while, say, three months, it would be misleading and even improper to show that you are still employed, so you should give your termination date. Due to the current volatility in health care, being unemployed is common. The stigma it bears is less than in years past. Nonetheless, be prepared to explain the circumstances of your termination in a positive way during the interview.

Question: I am so concerned about keeping my search confidential that I don't want to include the name of my current employer on my resume. What should I do?

Answer: If you work for an employer well known and highly regarded in your field, then you are missing one of the major advantages of having worked there. In any case, it would be very unusual to omit the name of your current employer, so I would recommend listing it.

Question: I rejoined a former employer after a two-year absence. How do I explain this on my resume?

Answer: You can handle this situation in one of two ways: (1) treat it as separate employment, or (2) indicate the gap with an asterisk and refer the reader to the section of the resume where the earlier employment is described.

Question: At one point in my career, I worked for an organization for only two months. Must I include that position on my resume?

Answer: Here the issue is disclosure. By not including this position, you risk damage to your integrity in the event that the reviewer or potential employer finds out about the position. But placing it in the section on employment would give it too much prominence. So include it briefly and matter-of-factly. One way to include the information without giving it equal importance with your other positions is to mark it with an asterisk near the end of your resume. Of course, if you are a recent graduate, include all the relevant summer jobs you have held.

Question: I have heard that placing my photograph on my resume is a good way to get attention. Is there any value added?

Answer: Absolutely not. A photograph on a resume is very unusual in the health care field; we are not in the entertainment or modeling business. As with other gimmicks, a photograph will make you stand out, but not in a professional way.

Tyler's Tip

Use action verbs in your writing. Verbs convey what you have done, what you are doing, and what you can do. And that is why people want to hire you—because you get things done. I suggest the following action verbs: chair, control, decrease, develop, direct, edit, establish, handle, implement, manage, negotiate, review, revise, supervise.

At the same time, cut out extra words by using verbs instead of nominalizations. For example, writing "implemented" instead of "conducted the implementation of" streamlines your resume. Also, avoid using the verbs "utilize" and "facilitate" because they do not specify concrete action.

Appendix 1.1

Example of a Historical Resume

RICHARD J. OVERACHIEVER, FACHE

1598 Madison Drive	(305) 555-0000 (Residence)
Lakeside, Florida 38138	(305) 555-9999 (Business)

EDUCATION
1972 **MHA**—Hospital Administration, George Washington University, Washington, D.C.
1968 **BS**—Business Administration, Clemson University, Clemson, South Carolina

EXPERIENCE
7/78 **METHODIST HEALTH MANAGEMENT, INC.,**
to Ocala, Florida
pres. (A nonprofit multihospital system with revenues of $210 million)
Vice President/Operations (4/82 to present)
Responsibilities: Management of 11 hospitals in three states with licensed complement of 1,700 beds. Serve on the Board of Directors of four facilities.
Accomplishments:
- Converted six hospitals from county ownership to Methodist Health Management ownership within a 12-month period.
- Established a purchasing program for the entire system that resulted in $2 million in first-year savings.
- Developed systemwide insurance programs for self-funding health insurance and life insurance.
- Reduced accounts receivable in all hospitals; implemented improved credit and collection policies and improved cash flow projections, resulting in $10 million cash flow improvements in 12 months.
- Developed the management engineering function at the corporate level in preparation for staffing reductions under prospective payment system.
- Processed six successful CONs and added four CT scanners and two digital subtraction angiography units for all hospitals.

Executive Director, Northside Memorial Hospital (7/78 to 4/82), Northside, Virginia (365 beds)

Responsibilities: Administrative management of the facility.

Accomplishments:

- Regained two-year accreditation four months after arrival; second two-year accreditation also granted.
- Developed first financial budget, personnel budget, and first capital equipment budget.
- Improved financial results from operating loss in FY 1975 to four years of successive improvements in operating margin; in FY 1980 the margin exceeded 5.5%.
- Refiled Medicare/Medicaid cost reports for 1973–1977 to restate depreciation schedules resulting in an additional $80,000 a year increase in reimbursement.
- Processed five successful CONs; prepared CON including coordination of financial feasibility for a $37 million replacement facility; worked with architects on development of program plan and block drawings.
- Developed and participated in physician recruitment program that added 23 physicians to a medical staff of 90.
- Added a data communication system that increased revenues by 6%.

7/76 to 7/78 **ST. ANTHONY'S HOSPITAL**, Beaumont, Louisiana (350 beds)

Administrator

Responsibilities: Administrative management of 18 departments.

Accomplishments:

- Established a Management Engineering Department that reported cost savings of $600,000 its first year.
- Led planning and construction of a $1.2 million expansion of the Nuclear Medicine Department.
- Participated in successful campaign against Teamsters Union effort to organize service and maintenance employees.
- Led planning, construction, and purchasing of one of the first full-body CT scanners installed in the country.

6/72   **MEDICAL CENTER OF FORT WORTH**, Fort Worth,
to   Texas
7/76   (350 beds with planning and expansion resulting in 500 beds)
        Associate Administrator (7/75 to 7/76)
        Responsibilities: Administrative management of 12 depart-
        ments as well as the utilization review function and malprac-
        tice litigation.
        Accomplishments:
        • Reorganized Outpatient Services to include establishment
          of a billing system.
        • Wrote utilization review plan and disaster plan.
        • Developed MBO project with Housekeeping Department.
        • Developed program for computerization of all purchasing
          functions.
        • Participated in the development of a long-range plan and
          the development of a $27 million expansion.

        Assistant Administrator (6/72 to 7/75)
        Responsibilities: Management of ancillary services and
        chairman of several committees.

PROFESSIONAL AFFILIATIONS

        American College of Healthcare Executives, Fellow since
            1982; Regent, 1984
        American Hospital Association
        Florida Hospital Association, Chairman (1982–1983)

OUTSIDE INTERESTS

        Tennis, golf, and snow skiing

REFERENCES

        Furnished upon request.

Appendix 1.2

Example of a Historical Resume with *Incorrect* Use of Dates

RICHARD J. OVERACHIEVER, FACHE

1598 Madison Drive	(305) 555-0000 (Residence)
Lakeside Florida 38138	(305) 555-9999 (Business)

EDUCATION

1972   **MHA**—Hospital Administration, George Washington University, Washington, D.C.

1968   **BS**—Business Administration, Clemson University, Clemson, South Carolina

EXPERIENCE

4/82   **METHODIST HEALTH MANAGEMENT, INC.,**
to   Ocala, Florida
pres. (A nonprofit multihospital system with revenues of $210 million)

Vice President/Operations (4/82 to present)

Responsibilities: Management of 11 hospitals in three states with licensed complement of 1,700 beds. Serve on the Board of Directors of four facilities.

Accomplishments:

- Converted six hospitals from county ownership to Methodist Health Management ownership within a 12-month period.
- Established a purchasing program for the entire system that resulted in $2 million in first-year savings.
- Developed systemwide insurance programs for self-funding health insurance and life insurance.
- Reduced accounts receivable in all hospitals; implemented improved credit and collection policies and improved cash

---

Note: Because the date is in the left margin, this resume makes the reader think that Richard had two different employers. When listing positions held within a single organization, even in separate locations, indicate the dates for each position immediately after the job description.

flow projections, resulting in $10 million cash flow improvements in 12 months.
- Developed the management engineering function at the corporate level in preparation for staffing reductions under prospective payment system.
- Processed six successful CONs and added four CT scanners and two digital subtraction angiography units for all hospitals.

7/78   *Executive Director, Northside Memorial Hospital,*
to   Northside, Virginia
4/82   (365 beds)
          Responsibilities: Administrative management of the facility.
          Accomplishments:
          - Regained two-year accreditation four months after arrival; second two-year accreditation also granted.
          - Developed first financial budget, personnel budget, and first capital equipment budget.

Appendix 1.3

Example of a Functional Resume

RICHARD J. OVERACHIEVER, FACHE

1598 Madison Drive	(305) 555-0000 (Residence)
Lakeside, Florida 38138	(305) 555-9999 (Business)

Career Objective:
To obtain a senior-level administrative position in a for-profit hospital in the Chicago area

Skills:

Financial

Reduced accounts receivables in all hospitals; implemented improved credit and collection policies and improved cash flow projections.

Developed first financial budget, first personnel budget, and first capital equipment budget.

Processed six successful CONs.

Established a Management Engineering Department that reported cost savings of $600,000 in its first year.

Managerial

Converted six hospitals from county ownership to Methodist Health Management ownership within a 12-month period.

Regained two-year accreditation four months after arrival; second two-year accreditation also granted.

Reorganized Outpatient Services to include establishment of a billing system.

Negotiating

Participated in successful campaign against Teamsters Union effort to organize service and maintenance employees.

Developed and participated in physician recruitment program that added 23 physicians to a medical staff of 90.

Employment:
Methodist Health Management, Inc., Ocala, Florida, 1978–present (including five years at one of its member institutions, Northside Memorial Hospital, Northside, Virginia)

St. Anthony's Hospital, Beaumont, Louisiana, 1976–1978

Medical Center of Fort Worth, Fort Worth, Texas, 1972–1976

Education:
George Washington University, Washington, D.C., MHA 1972

Clemson University, Clemson, South Carolina, BS 1968

Professional Affiliations:
American College of Healthcare Executives

American Hospital Association

Florida Hospital Association, Chairman (1982–1983)

Appendix 1.4
Example of a Narrative Resume

Richard J. Overachiever, FACHE
1598 Madison Drive
Lakeside, Florida 38138

I am currently the Vice President of Operations of Methodist Health Management, Inc., in Ocala, Florida. This nonprofit multihospital system has annual revenues of $210 million, and I am directly responsible for the management of its eleven member hospitals, which are located in Virginia, Florida, and Georgia, and have a licensed complement of 1700 beds. My accomplishments during my tenure are extensive: We converted six hospitals from county ownership to Methodist Health Management ownership over a twelve-month period, established a purchasing program for the entire system that contained costs quite effectively, implemented insurance programs for the entire system in the interest of uniformity, and conducted several CONs, which led to substantial expansion of our facilities.

Prior to my moving to Florida, I served as the Executive Director of one of Methodist Health Management's hospitals, Northside Hospital in Northside, Virginia. As a result of my efforts, we regained our two-year accreditation soon after my arrival. In addition, I developed Northside's first financial, personnel, and capital equipment budgets, as well as improving the hospital's financial performance from an operating loss in the mid-1970s to four years of successive improvements. As Executive Director, I developed the physician recruitment program that added many physicians to our medical staff.

I entered the health care administration field after completing my Master's of Health Administration at George Washington University in our nation's capital. My alma mater is Clemson University in South Carolina. Through my membership in the American College of Healthcare Executives, the American Hospital Association, and the Florida Hospital Association, I actively participate in the ongoing issues in our profession. My interests outside of my work include playing tennis, golf, and snow skiing when I can take the time to head north.

In summary, I am a highly motivated and experienced professional who can contribute significantly to your health care organization.

2

Cover Letters

An honest tale speeds best being plainly told.
—William Shakespeare

Cover letters are the most straightforward part of the job search process. Your cover letter should compel the reader to view the attached resume. Unfortunately, many people treat the cover letter as a creative writing exercise. They try to make the cover letter unique, but instead they end up making themselves look odd or eccentric—not usually viewed as positive attributes in the conservative world of health care. Avoid gimmicks. Keep in mind that the cover letter complements your resume; they work hand-in-hand to present you and your career goals in the most professional light.

Structure of the Cover Letter

This chapter will help you construct the three-paragraph cover letter. Do not deviate from this structure. After you familiarize yourself with the three-paragraph structure, you can customize each letter for the particular position in which you are interested. I have included examples of actual cover letters at the end of the chapter.

First Paragraph

The first paragraph of the cover letter should explain why you are writing. If, for example, you learned of the opening from a friend of the addressee, then you should mention that fact in the opening sentence. If you are responding to an ad you saw in a publication, then mention where you read the ad and specify the position that was advertised. In large organizations like hospitals and health care institutions, the opening sentence of your cover letter allows the reader to easily determine where to route your letter.

Second Paragraph

The second paragraph should detail your accomplishments, experience, or abilities and relate them to the job as you understand it. For example, if you are currently the assistant administrator of a facility and you are applying for a position as the COO of another facility, then you might note the many times when, in the administrator's absence, you were in charge of the day-to-day operations of the hospital. Or you might discuss your interaction with nursing services and your relationship with the physicians—two very important aspects of the COO job. On the other hand, because of the limits of space, you would not detail how you reorganized the security department. You would concentrate on the higher-level work and on those responsibilities that correspond to those of the COO.

Third Paragraph

The third paragraph should ask for two specific things: further consideration for this position and an interview. You should indicate your intent to follow up on your resume at a later date and actually do it. Following up shows genuine interest on your part and ensures that the right person has received your cover letter and resume.

One further item to consider including in the third paragraph is the salary level you seek. Different employment advisers have different views on this matter. Some recruiting experts argue that salary should be the very last subject that is introduced—following the interview—and certainly should not be mentioned in the cover letter. They argue that you should first get the hiring authority very interested in you before you discuss money because you will get a higher offer.

I disagree with this view. By mentioning salary, you avoid wasting your time and can focus on realistic prospects worth pursing. Say, for example, you are still employed while you are conducting your job search. The time you can be away from your job is limited. You only have so many vacation and personal days. Imagine that you go through a one- or two-day first interview, then a second interview, and only then learn that the position pays much less than you had anticipated and there is no room for negotiation. Now don't you wish you had introduced the issue of salary at the onset? You need not say exactly what you currently earn, but it is advisable to indicate the salary range that you seek.

But suppose you request a salary that is much less than the range for the position. Will the employer call your bluff, and if so, are you risking leaving "money on the table" in your negotiations? Perhaps, but more often than not, the salary you seek is a squeeze the employer can make. Based on my extensive experience in executive recruiting, I can assure you that negotiations more often result in a salary range being raised than in the employee leaving money on the table.

Proofreading the Cover Letter

Once you have completed your cover letter, proofread it for content. Does it include the most relevant information for that particular position? Have you carefully considered and explained why you are a qualified candidate? Have you expressed your interest in further discussing, that is, interviewing for, the position?

Now proofread it for quality. Have you corrected all grammatical mistakes, misspelled words, and typographical errors? In business correspondence, it is unconscionable for any letter to go out containing mistakes. At our office, as in most offices, some "smarty pants" will always circle a typo on circulating correspondence. Your business correspondence reflects your standards of professionalism. Print your cover letter on high-quality bond paper with a conventional typeface. Proofread it one final time for errors.

In particular, it is important that you double check the spelling of the name, title, and address of the person to whom you are writing. People expect their names to be spelled correctly and may be offended when they are misspelled. I have received numerous cover letters addressed to the anonymous "Sir." As a health care executive involved in a serious job search, you can certainly research a position and find out the name of the correct person to whom you should address your letter. Attending to this detail demonstrates your genuine interest in the position.

Cover Letters to Search Consultants

When you are writing a cover letter to executive search consultants, there are some special considerations. You are asking them to help you in locating employers who might be interested in your background. It is appropriate to include your current salary and your salary expectations, as well as your geographic preferences, because they need to know more about you in order to represent your interests. Also, include the types of positions in which you are interested and any special considerations, such as a working spouse. If it is important that you be contacted at home instead of your office, you should also include this information in your cover letter.

Examples of Cover Letters

Appendixes 2.1, 2.2, and 2.3 are examples of typical cover letters for someone applying for a job in health care. Use these as guides when you prepare your own cover letters. Notice that I said "cover letters"—you will need to write a new one for each position. Appendixes 2.4, 2.5, and 2.6 are negative examples. Notice how they violate the principles I have provided. Appendix 2.4 is too brief and fails to give any significant information pertaining to the actual position. Appendix 2.5 is not a letter, but rather a list of references; it also begins with a gimmicky paragraph. You definitely do not want to sound like a commercial announcer, as the writer does here. Similarly, Appendix 2.6 is an unsuccessful attempt to be catchy. (This particular example came from our in-house files; only the name has been changed). Compare these three letters with Appendixes 2.1, 2.2, and 2.3. Now compose a three-paragraph cover letter that is as straightforward and informative, and that will make the reader interested in you.

Appendix 2.1

Positive Example: Cover Letter in Response to an Advertisement

January 23, 1995

Thomas Sheridan
Vice President—Board of Trustees
Mercy Hospital
Upper Darby, PA 19433

Dear Mr. Sheridan:

I am writing in response to your job listing in the January 18 *National Employment Business Weekly*. Currently I am the COO for Connecticut Medical Center, where, as my enclosed resume details, I have served for the past five years.

At this point, I am interested in the greater challenges of a larger hospital. During my years at CMC, I oversaw two bond financings, negotiated an employee class-action suit that had threatened to shut down our facility, and increased our profitability by 24%, despite the fact that Bridgeport was especially hard hit by the recession.

The advertised position matches well with my background and professional goals. I would appreciate the chance to interview for the position. I will telephone you at the end of this week to discuss this further.

Sincerely yours,

Donald Stone

Appendix 2.2

Positive Example: Cover Letter to an
Executive Search Consultant

April 7, 1994

Mr. Joseph Connor
Dasey and Connor Healthcare Consultants
Minneapolis, MN 55401

Dear Mr. Connor:

I am writing to ask that your firm consider me as I pursue an advancement in hospital administration at the chief executive level. As I describe in my enclosed resume, I have a strong professional background and proven managerial skills. Your firm's national reputation as executive search consultants prompted me to ask that you consider me as a candidate.

As I detail in my resume, I presently serve as the acting CEO for the Shriners Hospital in Chicago. I have declined being named as CEO, for professional reasons, after serving in this position for the past six months. My current position has afforded me the chance to oversee our hospital become competitive, while decreasing our budget deficit by 85%. Nonetheless, I want to move on to a larger, profit-based organization, more of a hospital without walls, which can respond to the ongoing changes in health care delivery. My salary range is $120,000 to $140,000.

During the week of April 2, I will be in Minneapolis to attend the Midwest Conference of the American College of Healthcare Executives. I would welcome the opportunity to talk with you in person. I will call you this week to schedule an appointment.

Sincerely yours,

John P. Kelly

Appendix 2.3

Positive Example: Cover Letter for a Position Suggested by a Network Member

May 27, 1994

Mr. Martin Danahay
University Healthcare Associates
8 Oxford Place, Suite 3500
Columbia, South Carolina 29201

Dear Mr. Danahay:

My former college roommate, Laura Micinski-Colt, suggested that I contact you in reference to the Materials Management position currently available in your organization as listed in the *Southern Hospitals* classified section.

Following my graduation from the University of Florida's Graduate School of Public Health, I began working at Ocala Regional Medical Center as a purchasing agent. Since that time, I have reduced equipment costs by 18%, increased the use of competitive bidding with net savings to the bottom line of $650,000 per year, and completed my own database for inventory tracking.

I would greatly appreciate the opportunity to discuss my qualifications with you in person. I will call you next week. Thank you for your consideration.

Sincerely yours,

Elizabeth Rorty

Appendix 2.4

Negative Example:
The Short, Vague Cover Letter

September 9, 1994

Sandra Ohrbach
Director
Urgi-Care Medical Services, Inc.
Seattle, Washington 98109

Dear Ms. Ohrbach:

Enclosed please find my resume. I am interested in working for your organization. The state of Washington, Seattle in particular, has a fine reputation as a beautiful place to live and work.

I am currently seeking employment in hospital administration, am married with no children, and am a dependable worker.

Thank you for considering me for this position.

Sincerely yours,

Arthur Hodges

Appendix 2.5

Negative Example:
The Self-Advertisement Cover Letter

March 15, 1994

Jerome Kepes
Personnel Director
West Hills Hospital
Kalamazoo, Michigan 49001

Dear Mr. Kepes:

You have been unsuccessful in recruiting for your Budgeting Director, as I can see from the continued notices in the *Detroit Free Press*. *I* have a solution for your problem. The following people have the low-down on the right man for the job:

Professor Allen Michaelson, Accounting Department, Michigan State University

Sally Morrison, Vice-President of Finance, Detroit Suburban Hospital

Catherine Gibbs, M.D., Chief Resident, Detroit Suburban Hospital

Stephen Miller, President, Michigan Medical Supplies, Inc.

George Detweiler, Vice-President, First National Bank, Birmingham, Michigan

Contact any of these individuals for the straight scoop on my professional background and expertise. You will discover that *I am uniquely qualified* for the Budgeting Director position, soon-to-be filled, at West Hills Hospital.

I look forward to hearing from you.

Sincerely yours,

Timothy Burke

Appendix 2.6

Negative Example:
The Attention Grabbing Cover Letter

July 8, 1994

Mr. Larry Tyler
Tyler & Company
1000 Abernathy Road NE
Suite 1400
Atlanta, Ga 30328-5655

Dear Mr. Tyler:

Long ago, high up in the mountains of California, hardworking men searched for the gold that would make them rich. They panned the water and mined the earth without ceasing, in their search for gold. Very few ever found what they so steadfastly sought, yet they persevered in their mining for gold. These goldminers never doubted that they would ultimately find the priceless mineral that would change their lives. They toiled in the hope of someday striking gold.

Perhaps you are wondering at this point what the golden nugget is in this letter. Very simply, it is my resume. This document is just what you have been looking for. It gives you a golden opportunity to interview an individual who has proven to be invaluable to all of his employers.

Thank you for your consideration.

Sincerely yours,

John Gold

3

References

Good name in man and woman, dear my lord,
Is the immediate jewel of their souls.
—William Shakespeare

The reference list is the third part of the job search trilogy. Your reference list should be separate from your resume. Have your reference list ready before you start your job search so you won't be caught off guard when an interested party requests it. Take as much care in choosing your references and preparing the actual list as you do in preparing your resume and cover letters. These three items represent you to potential employers. Make sure that they do you credit.

Importance of References

What exact role do the references you list play in your job search? First, they provide an interviewer with the opportunity to obtain independent verification of the information that you have supplied. Second, they provide the person listed as a reference with the opportunity to sell you to your potential employer with a glowing report. If you have earned the respect of others in your professional life, you will have a ready pool of potential references who in all likelihood will be very happy to recommend you.

How important is the list of references? Most thoughtful and cautious employers will require a list of references and will conduct reference checks. Usually, the references are checked prior to an offer of employment. Occasionally, an offer is made contingent upon a satisfactory reference check. In either case, good solid references are an important part of the job change process.

Use of the Reference List

Use your references sparingly and judiciously. It is inappropriate to include the reference list when you send your cover letter and resume to a potential employer. The final item on your resume should say "References available upon request." Wait until a prospective employer asks for your list of references. This practice saves not only paper, but far more importantly, your time and the time of your references.

Do not attach letters of reference to your resume. Very few organizations require them. A letter of reference is an anachronism; you do not need to get one from an employer when you leave a job. Letters of reference are noted more for what they omit than for what they actually say. They sound like form letters and lack any hard information about your performance. Instead, most organizations rely on a telephone conversation with some or all of the individuals given in the reference list. By calling the right person, and asking the right questions about what kind of person you are and how you performed your responsibilities, an interested employer will find out the information they need.

The Hierarchy of References

References can be divided into four categories, which should be prioritized as follows: supervisors, peers, subordinates, and others. The best references are supervisors, those people to whom you have reported in your work. List supervisors from up to ten years ago as references. Prospective employers will look very favorably on someone who pleased former supervisors.

Peers are those individuals with whom you have worked during your career. For example, if you are the vice president of nursing, the vice president of finance would be a logical choice to supply as a reference because that person can address your day-to-day performance. References from peers are a useful alternative if you are unable to obtain a positive reference from a supervisor because of a personality conflict or if a supervisor has died or cannot be located.

If you have alluded to a personality conflict with a former supervisor, a peer can attest to your assertions about the difficulty of working with that individual.

Subordinates are those people who have reported to you at some point. They are especially good references when the search committee includes potential subordinates, or when the hiring committee wants to determine an individual's management style. References from subordinates are particularly important when the organization values participatory management.

Others who can supply references to your character and work ethic are people who were not part of the management team at your former position, but are familiar with your work. For example, if you have worked as the chief financial officer, you could list the partner or senior manager of the auditing firm conducting the hospital's audit as a reference. Often, consultants and fellow professionals with whom you have served on a committee can provide a reference. A word of caution—do not misuse this category. Too often, earnest candidates name as references people whom they know only as acquaintances. Refrain from listing references simply because they have a national reputation when they have very little personal knowledge of your own situation. These references are often hard to contact, and their peripheral knowledge of you leads to a meaningless reference. You will then be looked upon as a "name dropper." List only those references with whom you have had active and direct professional contact.

Obtaining Permission from References

No matter which category they fall under, clear your references in advance. One of the biggest mistakes made by candidates is failing to talk to references ahead of time and not seeking their permission to be used as references. When you have chosen a possible reference, contact that individual and ask if he or she is willing to be a reference on your behalf. How you approach a potential reference is important. Don't tell them that you want them to be a reference for you; ask them whether they would feel comfortable about being placed in that position.

There are two reasons for asking permission of your references in advance. First, by asking, you may discern what kind of recommendation that person is likely to give. If the person assures you that he or she is happy to oblige you and seems enthusiastic about helping you, you probably can count on a strong reference from that person. Second, being a reference can require a great deal of time and some inconvenience. Asking in advance is a courtesy you should extend to the people you hope will recommend you.

Checking References

One good thing to do is to check your own references. You need to have a feel for what your references say about you so that you can address any issues brought up by the reference with your potential employer. Usually you can check your own references by asking directly of people who have called the reference what the reference had to say. Many times, the person will be willing to share the "meat" of the reference with you. Sometimes a personal friend who is also a potential employer may share the reference with you, or you may enlist the aid of a friendly search consultant to make inquiries. If you are fair and nonconfrontational, the references themselves will often tell you what they intend to say when people call. However you manage to learn what your references will say about you, this information will prepare you to deal with any negatives during the interview.

Composing the Reference List

After you have received permission from your references, you can compose your reference list. The actual list should include five or six people from the hierarchy of references. Ideally, you might list all of your former supervisors, up to six. If you cannot use your current supervisor for any reason, try to find someone within your organization who fits into one of the other three categories to serve as one of your references. Prospective employers will use your reference list to learn about your work history, so limit your choices to people who can concretely comment on what you have done and how well you have done it.

For each individual, list the correct name, title, office address, and business phone number. In addition, note in what capacity you know the reference. This information clears up any confusion that would result if some of your references have changed jobs, making their connection with your employment history difficult to discern. See Appendix 3.1 for an example of a reference list.

When we make reference checks at Tyler & Company on behalf of our clients, we find that typically references do not tell concerned parties everything. At times, we have to pull information out of them. As executive search consultants, we like to find very enthusiastic references who assure us of the candidate's caliber and the quality of his or her job performance. The more enthusiastic, the better. Some references "damn with faint praise."

Back Door References

You may be familiar with "back door" reference checks. A back door reference is one that you have not supplied to the prospective employer. In your job search, it is quite possible—indeed probable— that someone, at some point in the process, will conduct a back door reference check on you. A back door reference check can potentially be good or bad. On the one hand, the person whom the prospective employer contacts could speak highly of you, reinforcing whatever you have said. On the other hand, if you have not been candid, the back door reference could supply information that throws doubt upon your honesty and integrity.

Our company has a policy that we will not conduct back door reference checks on candidates if the possibility exists that it will jeopardize their current positions. If we have been unable to conduct reference checks with an appropriate set of references, then we always make the offer contingent upon receiving a final satisfactory reference from candidate's current supervisor.

Personal References

References from your pastor or personal references from your friends are neither necessary nor encouraged. One possible exception would be if you were pursuing a lead with an organization that has some religious affiliation; then the cleric's reference could strengthen your case. Generally, almost every piece of necessary and pertinent information can be obtained from the professional references furnished by you in your list of references.

Involving Your Current Employer

Before concluding this chapter, I want to discuss the most often asked question surrounding the issue of references: At what point do you tell your current boss that you are looking for a new position? Obviously, you would like to be able to involve your current boss in the job change process as long as your honesty does not hurt your present position. If you have alerted your supervisor that you are in the job search process, there is no lying or stretching the truth when you need to go away for an interview. Also, if you don't alert your boss, the possibility of your boss finding out that you are looking is still very high; it is easier to be upfront than to have the person learn of your plans from someone else.

Involving your supervisor in your job change process, however, carries certain risks. If the process lasts overly long, your supervisor may decide at some point that it is time for you to move along and impose a timetable on your job change. This situation can be extremely dangerous, especially in a down employment market. In some organizations, the announcement of a job search can be construed as a sign of disloyalty, and the individual is moved out of the organization almost immediately.

You must weigh your decision on involving your current employer in your job search based upon your knowledge of the organization and your relationship with your supervisor. In the ideal situation, your relationship with your supervisor will allow you to conduct your job search for the year or longer it might take in order for you to find an opportunity. Some candidates have found it helpful to remind a supervisor of his or her own career situation when having this conversation. Generally, if you are a talented and motivated employee, your supervisor will, however reluctantly, be cooperative in your job search.

Appendix 3.1

Example of a Reference List

Reference List for John Smith

Clifford Sunnarborg   **(215) 378-2888**
Retired
c/o Penn Financial Services
2900 Penn Street
Philadelphia, PA 19000
Worked as my immediate supervisor when I was an accountant at Drexel University.

Mark Herschberger C.P.A.   **(215) 614-9876**
Senior Partner
Hershberger and Company
100 Market Street, Suite 200
Philadelphia, PA 19000
Worked as my immediate supervisor when I was employed by Arthur Anderson.

Elaine Fenwick   **(215) 766-1234**
Director
Managed Health Care
1200 South Broad Street
Philadelphia, PA 19000
Worked as my immediate supervisor during my internship at Presbyterian Hospital.

Allan B. Cranmer   **(414) 938-8500**
Chief Operating Officer
Suburban General Hospital
655 Amberson Place
Milwaukee, WI 53201
Worked as my immediate supervisor while I was a financial analyst at Presbyterian Hospital.

Francis X. McCrory   **(213) 355-4321**
Vice President
San Luis Obispo University Health System (SLOUHS)
760 Center Avenue
San Luis Obispo, CA 91355
Worked as my immediate supervisor when I was accounting manager
at SLOUHS.

Ernest R. Talmadge   **(703) 893-3456**
Chair of the Board of Trustees
Houston City Hospital
355 South Street
Houston, TX 77328
Supervises me in my present position as vice president at Houston
City Hospital.

Part II

Making Contacts

4

Networking

Network or not work.
—Stephen Rosen

Networking has four objectives:

1. To locate a job opportunity
2. To be referred to someone who might have a job opportunity
3. To find out additional information
4. To ask for advice and counsel

Of these four, the first two are the most important. Keep these objectives in mind as you network.

The cynical adage "It's who you know" is a fact of life in any job search. It is particularly apt in the field of health care, but I would rephrase it as "It's who knows you." The best way to become known and respected in your field is by doing your job well. Your active participation in your profession serves as the basis of your network. In this chapter, I will first offer ways to find names for your network, and then, in the second half, show you how to use the Tyler Networking Technique (TNT) to put the contacts into an efficient system. TNT will allow you to keep track of whom you have contacted, when you contacted them, to whom you were referred, and what, if any, further steps need to be taken. You can enter this data base on your home computer, or use the forms that we provide at the end of the chapter.

Networking is an important part of your career, even if you are not currently seeking a new position. Networking, which in the broadest sense is the maintaining of active friendships with your professional colleagues, helps you to stay current with developments in health care across the country. By sharing your problems and successes, you can learn from others. When you eventually do undertake a job search, you will have a group of allies who will let you know of upcoming opportunities. They may also speak on your behalf or warn you if a particular position involves any problems, such as a tough board of directors.

Building a Network

Networking has become a commonplace term in career strategy literature, but few people know how to build a strong network for their own job search in any logical manner. Productive networking requires ongoing efforts to acquaint yourself with your fellow hospital administrators and business leaders. There are several sources for building your own network:

- College and graduate school class members
- Professional associations
- Professional conferences
- Professional journals
- Former co-workers and employees

In addition, you have the beginnings of a great network right at your desk. Use your Rolodex, your address book, and your collection of business cards to get the names of your first round of network contacts.

In your present job, keep a record of the names, positions, and addresses of the influential individuals whom you meet or whose work you respect. Make a point of maintaining contact with them by telephone or mail on an annual basis. For example, say you speak with a particularly accomplished attorney in the health care field at your class reunion and you exchange business cards. Although that person may live on the other coast, telephone him or her a month or so after the reunion and say how much you enjoyed your conversation. Discuss a current issue and ask for the person's opinion. This phone call builds an acquaintance with a dynamic person, who is actively involved in health care, and sows a seed for your network.

Your demanding work schedule may preclude you from attending seminars and conferences every month, but you owe it to yourself to attend at least two conferences per year. The American College of Healthcare Executives typically schedules Eastern, Western, and executive sessions annually. Its annual Congress on Administration is especially productive. Make time for one of them every year. Not only will attending conferences give you a new perspective and keep you apprised of current issues, but you will also have a chance to catch up with old friends and make new ones.

Another way to network without leaving your office is by subscribing to and reading professional journals. Keep track of career moves via *Healthcare Executive's* "Focus On" feature, which addresses the concerns of health care executives in every third issue. The "Professional Development Calendar" provides a schedule of upcoming meetings across the country. In *Modern Healthcare's Weekly Business News*, the following three features regularly provide useful information: "Professional Exchange," "Career Opportunities," and "Calendar/People." Another publication, *AHA News*, features a section called "Personal Update," which also tracks the career moves of health care professionals. By reading these features, you can keep track of who is working where and when upcoming meetings are scheduled. Staying informed is an important part of networking.

Staying involved also contributes to the strength of your network. For example, when you read a thought-provoking article in one of your professional journals, you should copy it and send it to people who might be interested in it. This is one way to interact with other health care executives whom you rarely have an opportunity to see, but with whom it may be worth your while to maintain contact.

Throughout your career, you will meet people with whom you share similar interests and goals. Your former employees and co-workers, especially the hard-working and ambitious ones, are an excellent source of potential members for your network. Stay in touch with them after either they or you leave your organization. You will have contacts in many organizations, each of whom, in turn, knows several other people who are themselves potential contacts.

Expand your network by including professionals in related fields like physicians, attorneys, and health care recruiters. Civic and business leaders tend to know a great many people. The more varied and extensive the membership, the more useful your network may be when you are conducting your job search.

One common-sense reminder when building a network: We are often judged by the company we keep. Just because someone holds a very responsible position does not qualify that person for your network. Does that individual have the integrity you require? I remember reading about a hospital administrator who served time for embezzling funds from his hospital. Nice guy, but a crook nevertheless. Admittedly, it is difficult to tell if someone is capable of stealing, but be alert to clues about a person's character. Invest the time it takes in maintaining contact only when the person passes that subjective test. Another consideration is whether or not you like and trust the person. Can you count on this person passing on helpful information to you if the need arises?

Just as networking computers increases their power, networking professionally increases your working capacity, expands your sphere of influence, and connects you with others who share similar concerns and goals. If you include networking in your workday, not only will you have opportunities to discuss work-related issues regardless of whether you are in the job market, but you are storing up goodwill chits to call in if the need arises.

Two hundred years ago, long before the notion of career development and its specific vocabulary existed, the eminent lexicographer Samuel Johnson defined "network" as "any thing reticulated or decussated at equal distances, with interstices between the intersections." An "interstice" is a space that intervenes between two objects. Think of your contact as an interstice who can intervene on your behalf, and move you to the next intersection. When you contact someone and obtain even one new name to contact in your job search, that contact, or interstice, has been useful.

Networking brings results. Stephen Rosen, an astrophysicist and career counselor who works with professionals from the former Soviet Union, tells his clients unfamiliar with the American business culture to "network or not work." It's that simple.

Networking Techniques

I have watched hundreds of people network their way into new jobs. It has been interesting to see how effectively some individuals network, and how ineptly others try to network. Therefore, at this point, I want to offer some of the networking techniques that I use as a search consultant that can be transferred to your job search. If you think about it for a minute, it makes sense. As a search consultant, what I do is to network with potential candidates and centers of influence in order to locate a number of interested and qualified candidates. What you are doing is using the same technique in reverse.

Here are some key words in networking that we have to get down before we begin.

1. "Help"
2. "Please"
3. "If you don't mind"
4. "Thank you"

In his book on personal marketing strategies, Mike McCaffrey talks about his technique for incorporating these expressions into your networking efforts.[1] McCaffrey is right on target. Almost everyone with whom you have contact will want to help you in your job search. Many will have had a similar experience and, as a result, will be able to relate to your circumstances. You are not imposing on their time, but you are giving them an opportunity to put a little something back into society. Most people will be willing to give you a bit of their time and talk to you.

No matter how uncomfortable you feel at first, don't be shy or reluctant to call strangers and talk to them about relevant names and opportunities for you. Some of the most delightful conversations I have ever had have been while networking and talking to an interesting, friendly person.

Talking with Secretaries

Contacting potential employers and centers of influence can be quite difficult at times because many secretaries have been taught to screen callers in order to eliminate sales calls. I have found it advantageous to go ahead and announce my name to the secretary right up front.

Secretary: "Mr. Johnson's office, Mary Smith speaking."

Tyler: "Mary, this is Larry Tyler. Is Bill in?"

Most of the time I will be put right through to Mr. Johnson. Surprisingly, the direct approach most often works.

Occasionally, the secretary will ask the nature of your call. How you handle this question will determine whether you will get a return call or not. See what you think of this continuation of my phone call to Bill Johnson.

Secretary: "I'm sorry, Mr. Tyler, but Mr. Johnson is not in today. May I leave him a message?"

Tyler: "Certainly. Please have him call me at (404) 396-3939. I'll be in all week."

Secretary: "And Mr. Tyler, may I tell him the nature of the call?"

Tyler: "Yes, you may. I am currently in the process of networking in order to identify new job opportunities. I was . . . " Here you choose one of the following:

1. "referred to Mr. Johnson by Jane Smith of Humana"
2. "referred to Mr. Johnson by several people in the profession"
3. "told that Mr. Johnson was an influential individual, well respected within health care"

"Given Mr. Johnson's position, I don't want to waste his time, but I could certainly use his advice and counsel as I am networking. If I could only have ten minutes of his time, I would be very appreciative."

Secretary: "Very well, Mr. Tyler. I will give him your message."

Tyler (oozing with sincerity): "Thank you so much, Mary. I know you get a lot of calls like this, but I appreciate your attention and professionalism. I hope you will use your influence with Mr. Johnson to get us connected."

Secretary: "I'll surely do my best. Good-bye."

Now I make a mental and written note of Mr. Johnson's secretary. Every time I call in order to talk with Mr. Johnson, I remember to acknowledge her and treat her with courtesy and respect. She is the gatekeeper to Mr. Johnson and a potential ally in my search.

Be especially nice to secretaries because they are the confidants of the boss.

Talking with a New Network Contact

When you finally reach Mr. Johnson, McCaffrey's technique of using the magic words will be especially beneficial. Remember to include the key words "please" and "thank you" throughout your conversation. Here is how your phone call to Johnson might go:

Tyler: "Mr. Johnson, thank you for returning my call. As I told your secretary, I was referred to you by (fill in the blank). I am in the process of changing positions and am seeking your (any of the following: advice, counsel, input, suggestions) as to opportunities that might exist for a person with my background and abilities. If this is a bad time for you, please let me know and we can schedule a call for a better time. I don't want to interfere with anything you might have going on, but if you can help me, I would really appreciate it."

Johnson: "Well, I have a couple minutes. Go ahead."

Tyler: "Thank you so much."

Then proceed to tell him briefly about yourself and the type of position that interests you. You do not ask Mr. Johnson if that type of position is open in his organization because you want his referrals and advice first. How your conversation progresses will depend on how much time Mr. Johnson wants to spend and what kind of rapport you establish on the phone. You should get the names of several people Mr. Johnson thinks might either have an opening or who might be good network leads.

Tyler: "Mr. Johnson, I really appreciate your help with these referrals. Is it all right if I tell these referrals where I got their names?"

In most cases, the person will permit you to use his or her name, but you must get permission. You need to make sure that you follow Mr. Johnson's directions, because in some cases, his name might be a negative. For example, I have often told networking candidates about a position that one of my competitors was recruiting for. If the candidate had mentioned my name, it would have caused suspicion that might have hurt that person's chances.

As the conversation winds down, remember to do three things. First, volunteer to send the person a copy of your resume. If Mr. Johnson volunteers the address, then write it down. Otherwise, if you don't have the address, call Ms. Smith back later and get it from her, along with the correct spelling of his name and his correct title. Second, see what kind of follow-up Mr. Johnson might expect. Will he be interested to know the results of your conversation with his referral? If so, ask if you can call him in a week or two to let him know. This opportunity to talk again with Mr. Johnson may prove helpful because he may have other suggestions or opportunities he has come up with in the mean time. Third, close the conversation.

Tyler: "Mr. Johnson, you have been so helpful. I don't know how I can thank you enough for your time and advice."

Johnson: "Don't think anything of it. I was glad to help."

Tyler: "Good-bye now."

Tyler Networking Technique (TNT)

Now that you are convinced of the importance of networks and prepared to build a network of interstices and intersections that will lead to your new job, you need a system to manage this unwieldy web of information. The Tyler Networking Technique (TNT) has been developed at our company over the years, in response to candidates' need for a systematic way to keep track of their contacts. TNT has one purpose—to organize your network dynamically.

Here is how TNT works. Photocopy the form at the end of this chapter (Appendix 4.1), or use your computer to record the same information. On the first record, fill in the correct information, including the person's name, his or her company, title, and telephone number. Then complete the items in the left-hand margin: reference number, referred by, the reference number of the referral, and whether or not you may use the referral name.

You then contact the person, in most cases, by telephone. Take notes during the conversation and then complete the TNT record. The purpose of this form is to note the outcome. What leads did you obtain? What further action do you need to take? To whom did this individual refer you? In Appendix 4.2, you can see an example of TNT in action. By consistently and methodically using this record-keeping system, you can manage the information instead of relying on scraps of paper, your cluttered address book, business cards, or worst of all, your memory. Although all those sources give you names, the record keeping gives you control.

The TNT system can be used with a calendar that functions as a "tickler" for your memory. When a lead develops, or someone says, "Call me back later," you will need to mark your calendar to follow up with the promised action on the appointed date.

Now let's go through how the TNT forms are completed. Please note that each entry has a number. A good goal is to make contact with at least 500 potential employers or centers of influence—people who are able to refer you to potential employers by virtue of their job or place in the health care field. Examples of centers of influence include the following:

- the regional AHA representative
- the president of the state hospital association
- the chair of the board of the state hospital association
- the departmental chair of an academic program in hospital administration
- the president of the state HFMA chapter
- the president of AONE

Begin by placing the names of people you already know on the TNT forms. Fill in all the information required by the forms and start making phone calls. After each phone call, record your comments and "ticklerize" any dates for follow-up calls. If you are referred to another individual, begin a separate TNT record for that person. Be sure to include the name of the person who referred you to that next individual, and whether it is okay to use the first person's name. As you undertake this systematic networking, you will find that many people are happy to give you information and leads, but wish to keep their names out of the process. You must honor such requests, which are usually motivated by a wish for privacy.

Sometimes you may end up obtaining a referral to another individual within the same organization. When this happens, you might want to group your contacts from that organization together, reducing duplication of effort. Go back to the TNT record for the first contact in the organization. Let's say it is #14. Number that contact "14A" and the new contact "14B." By adding the letter, you cue yourself that you have more than one contact with that company. Your next contact in the same organization is, of course, 14C. The objective is to maintain clear, organized records that you can use.

In the interests of good record keeping, assemble your TNT worksheets in a three-ring binder. Place any correspondence immediately after the respective TNT contact sheet. Staple any business cards to the contact sheet. As you work the phones, document every step so that your efforts are not misplaced.

In the course of your job search, your network will expand in number and size, but you can control it and keep track of your networking efforts by using TNT. Even after you have established yourself in your new position, maintain this record. Not only will you be able to return the favor of being a helpful contact, but you will not have to reinvent the wheel in the event of a future job search.

Note

1. Michael McCaffrey, *Personal Marketing Strategies* (Englewood Cliffs, NJ: Prentice-Hall, 1983), 30.

Appendix 4.1

TNT Worksheet

Tyler Networking Technique©

Reference #:	NAME:	TITLE:		
	COMPANY:	PHONE: ( )		
Referred by:				
Ref. # of Referral:				
OK to Refer?		FOLLOW-UP:		
Reference #:	NAME:	TITLE:		
	COMPANY:	PHONE: ( )		
Referred by:				
Ref. # of Referral:				
OK to Refer?		FOLLOW-UP:		
Reference #:	NAME:	TITLE:		
	COMPANY:	PHONE: ( )		
Referred by:				
Ref. # of Referral:				
OK to Refer?		FOLLOW-UP:		

Appendix 4.2

Example of a TNT form in Progress

Tyler Networking Technique ©

Reference #:		
6	NAME: *Michael Anderson*	TITLE: *Director*
Referred by:	COMPANY: *Healthcare Associates*	PHONE: *(215) 612-1000 x 57*
Bob Smith	*Suite 200 The Franklin Building Philadelphia PA 19193*	
Ref. # of Referral:	*3/12/94 Referenced following contacts: #9 Sr. Margaret Booth, S.C. #10 James Carpenter, J.D.*	
2	*#11 William Frazier, M.D.*	
OK to Refer?		
Y		FOLLOW-UP: *None*
Reference #:		
7	NAME: *Barbara Lieberman*	TITLE: *Budget Director*
Referred by:	COMPANY: *Northeastern Health Svce. Mgmt.*	PHONE: *(201) 498-6400*
self	*205 Adams Pkwy Boston MA 03071*	
Ref. # of Referral:	*3/12/94 Currently downsizing operations in New England—very bleak outlook.*	
—	*Did request dossier (classmate from grad school).*	
OK to Refer?		
Y		FOLLOW-UP: *Mail dossier 3/13/94.*
Reference #:		
8	NAME: *Bruce Krieger*	TITLE: *VP-Finance*
Referred by:	COMPANY: *Asbury Home Infusion*	PHONE: *(215) 707-2226*
self	*On vacation. CB next Week (Met him 5 yrs ago when working on AHA Mid-Atlantic Planning Cmte.)*	
Ref. # of Referral:		
—		
OK to Refer?		
Y		FOLLOW-UP: *3/20/94*

Reference #: 9	NAME: *Margaret Booth, SC. R.N.*	TITLE: *COO*
	COMPANY: *Sisters of Charity Hospital*	PHONE: *(412) 682-9393*
Referred by: *Mike Anderson*	*125 Forbes Ave. Pgh PA 15215*	
	3/12/94 Leave of absence til beginning of April (medical).	
Ref. # of Referral: *6*		
OK to Refer? *N/A*		FOLLOW-UP: *4/2/94*

Reference #: 10	NAME: *James Carpenter, J.D.*	TITLE: *Partner*
	COMPANY: *Pearson Matthews & Klein P.C.*	PHONE: *(312) 911-8400*
Referred by: *Mike Anderson*	*125 Lake Shore Drive, Chicago, IL 60601*	
	3/16/94 One of his associates (#12) Mark Koenig has an in w/ Director of Cedars Sinai Board,	
Ref. # of Referral: *6*	*(#13) Walter Abercrombie*	
	Referred: #14 Dorothea Myerson	
OK to Refer? *Y*	*#15 Roy Cullaney*	FOLLOW-UP: *3/23/94*

Reference #: 11	NAME: *William Frazier, M.D. (Red)*	TITLE: *Medical Director*
	COMPANY: *Health USA*	PHONE: *(301) 655-3200*
Referred by: *Mike Anderson*	*500 Charles St. Balto MD 21201*	
	3/16/94 His consulting firm has regional offices nationwide. Agreed to review my dossier.	
Ref. # of Referral: *6*	*Mailed 3/17/94*	
OK to Refer? *N*		FOLLOW-UP: *3/23/94*

Reference #: 12	NAME: *Mark Koenig, J.D.*	TITLE: *Associate*
Referred by: *J. Carpenter*	COMPANY: *Pearson, Matthews & Klein*	PHONE: *(312) 911-8440*
Ref. # of Referral: 10	*125 Lake Shore Drive Chicago IL 60601*	
	3/16/94 Extremely helpful. Gave me Walter Abercrombie's phone # and permission to use his name.	
OK to Refer? *Y*		FOLLOW-UP: *None*

Reference #: 13	NAME: *Walter Abercrombie*	TITLE: *Chair*
Referred by: *Mark Koenig*	COMPANY: *Board of Trustees—*	PHONE: *(212) 870-6100*
Ref. # of Referral: 12	*Cedar Sinai Medical Center NY NY 10012*	
OK to Refer? *Y*		FOLLOW-UP:

Reference #: 14	NAME: *Dorothea Myerson (Dot)*	TITLE: *VP, Exec Search*
Referred by: *J. Carpenter*	COMPANY: *O'Connor & Associates*	PHONE: *(414) 398-6800*
Ref. # of Referral: 10	*7000 Market Street Milwaukee, WI 53215*	
	3/18/94 Bingo! Currently she's retained in a search for a COO—500-bed n-p facility in Minneapolis.	
OK to Refer? *Y*		FOLLOW-UP: *Mail dossier 3/20/94.*
		Call on 3/22/94.

Reference #: 15	NAME: *Roy Cullaney*	TITLE: *Professor*
Referred by: *J. Carpenter*	COMPANY: *University of Chicago*	PHONE: *(312) 481-2110*
Ref. # of Referral: *10*	*Graduate School of Public Health 75 University Ave. Chicago IL 60320*	
	3/20/94 On semester break—returns next week. Tied in to ACHE (former member of Board of Governors—knows <u>everyone</u> apparently).	
OK to Refer? *N/A*	FOLLOW-UP: *3/28/94—C/B*	

Reference #:	NAME:	TITLE:
Referred by:	COMPANY:	PHONE: ( )
Ref. # of Referral:		
OK to Refer?	FOLLOW-UP:	

Reference #:	NAME:	TITLE:
Referred by:	COMPANY:	PHONE: ( )
Ref. # of Referral:		
OK to Refer?	FOLLOW-UP:	

5

Outplacement Firms

Every calamity is a spur and a valuable hint.
—Ralph Waldo Emerson

With the dismissal of health care executives and the "rightsizing" of operations in the field, there has been rapid growth in the number of outplacement firms with expertise in health care. Outplacement firms work with employees to make the transition to a new job. Their sole responsibility is to advise, counsel, prepare, and sometimes cajole the employee as his or her search progresses. More and more employers are offering outplacement services to displaced employees, primarily for two reasons. First, there are often far more candidates for positions in health care than there are jobs available. Employers know that it is not uncommon to have 300–400 applicants for one position, and competing for jobs takes time and expertise. An outplacement firm offers expertise and saves time for the candidates. Second, letting someone go after they have served an organization faithfully is a traumatic experience for all parties concerned. By drawing on the services of an outplacement firm, organizations try to soften the blow to both the displaced employee and the employees who remain. Morale stays higher because the displaced employee feels better and the remaining employees can see that the employee who left was treated fairly. Particularly in the midst of downsizing, employers cannot afford to have many disgruntled current or former employees saying bad things about the organization.

Often the roles of outplacement firms and executive search firms are confused. An outplacement firm works on behalf of the job seeker by helping him or her seek employment, while the executive search firm works on behalf of the employer who is seeking candidates. Although executive search firms often switch into the career counseling mode in order to be of help to a candidate, their first loyalty is to the employer, so the time they devote to career counseling is extremely limited. It might seem natural for search firms to provide outplacement services, but reputable executive search firms try to avoid doing outplacement because it creates an inherent conflict of interest. It is unethical for a firm to represent clients with competing interests. A similar conflict of interest occurs if outplacement firms try to take on the role of a search firm, so keeping the distinction between the two types of activities is extremely important.

Outplacement firms refer to the employer who is paying the fee for their services as the *sponsor*. Outplacement consultants often refer to themselves as *career counselors*, which has a more positive connotation than *outplacement consultant*. In this chapter, the two terms are used interchangeably.

What are the services that an individual can expect from an outplacement or career counseling firm? Among the services offered are the following:

- Resume preparation
- Practice interviews using a videotape
- Psychological testing
- Skill testing
- Access to secretarial help and sample form letters
- Access to research on various employers
- Networking
- Direct mail services
- Access to publications, directories, and other reference material
- Counseling
- Checking of references
- Business cards and stationery
- Job leads

Counseling may be the most important of the services offered. Outplacement counselors need to be among the most patient and people-sensitive humans on the planet. They associate daily with people who are going through traumatic times, so they must deal with bruised egos and help reestablish self-esteem. They they must work through months of the ups and downs of a candidate's job search. A candidate can be greatly influenced and his or her job search made easier by the abilities and insight of the career counselor.

How does one go about picking an outplacement counselor? In many cases, the employer has already lined up an outplacement specialist to deal with employees' transition out of the organization. This may be unfortunate for the employee, since ideally the employee should have some say in the selection of the outplacement firm. The employee needs to feel (on a personal level) that the firm really has his or her interests at heart. Nevertheless, the selection of the firm should not be left entirely to the discretion of the employee. The employer too should have input, since it is generally the employer that foots the bill for the service. In addition, employees may not know how to assess outplacement firms, whereas a knowledgeable human resources executive may have insight into an outplacement firm's track record in the market. The choice of an outplacement firm should be a joint one, with the employer negotiating the financial agreement before the final selection is made.

When selecting an outplacement firm, employees and employers should look for these things:

1. *A comprehensive list of services.* If you compare firms, you can see which one offers the types of services you need. Look for innovative services that may indicate a "cutting edge" firm. Basic services such as resume preparation can be obtained from other sources, including this book.

2. *Satisfied customers.* Ask to speak to successful candidates who have completed the program and found another job. Call three and find out what they have to say about the program and the counselors. Ask what they liked least and most about the program. Also, ask if they would select the same firm if they had to do it all over again. Then ask for the name of one other person who went through the program. Call that person for a "back door" reference on the firm.

3. *Specialization in health care.* Firms that are experienced in health care will provide more beneficial counseling and will have more health care references and referral sources in their library. In addition, you may have the opportunity to network

with other displaced executives in health care. I was amazed when I found out that one of the candidates I was working with had a list of all the assignments that our firm was working on, some of which were confidential. How did he get this list? It was compiled by a network of clients of the outplacement firm. Every time someone found out about a job, they put it on the list for others to use.

4. *Counseling experience.* How many clients do counselors have at one time? What did they do before doing this kind of work? What kind of educational background do they have? Why do they think they can do a better job of serving you than other counselors would?

Before you make the decision on the firm and the individual counselor, ask yourself one final set of questions. Are you the type of person who needs a motivational kick in order to work hard? Or do you respond better to coddling and warm encouragement? Outplacement counselors occasionally need to be a friend with a listening ear and occasionally a first sergeant who gives orders and accepts no excuses. Your career counselor should be able to be either of these, depending on what you need at any given time. I have watched too many candidates sit at home and do nothing when they should have been making phone calls. I have also watched candidates spend valuable months in exploring avenues that felt good but would undoubtedly end in a less than adequate outcome. Because the circumstances of your job search are most likely not of your choosing, and because you may have unresolved emotions about losing your job, the outplacement counselor needs to be sensitive to your feelings and skilled in helping you channel your emotional energy into your job search. Given the restructuring that is going on in health care, it is unlikely that all health care executives who are out of work will be able to find jobs in the field. An outplacement counselor should also have the knowledge, strength, and interpersonal skills to be able to tell a client that he or she will not find a job in health care and to help the client identify other career options. This is the ultimate test of an effective outplacement firm.

Appendix 5.1 is a directory of nationally recognized outplacement firms. It is not an exhaustive list, and it is not meant to endorse the companies listed, but it might help you get started on selecting a firm in your area.

Once you have selected an outplacement firm, you can expect the first few weeks of your work to be fairly intense since a number of activities have to be undertaken simultaneously. You will be preparing your resume, going through training classes on how to network, taking psychological texts, and practicing your interviewing skills. You will also be preparing lists of contacts and putting your plan together. Some outplacement firms offer office space and secretarial support in their offices, and you will be encouraged to come in every day to work on your search. Most candidates understand that this is only a temporary measure and that they need to have a permanent job. Don't get too comfortable going to the outplacement firm's office! The sooner you are in a permanent position, the better. A number of outplacement firms suggest that you work out of your home so that you will be constantly reminded that you need a job. This eliminates the tendency to deceive yourself by going to your temporary office. If you decide to work out of your home, make sure that the outplacement firm has a regular program of follow-up to see how you are doing.

Because of the sheer numbers of displaced executives and employees in health care, many businesses establish their own internal outplacement organization or contract with outsiders to do outplacement counseling and training for groups of employees. Under these arrangements, you are less likely to be offered the services of an individual counselor. Take advantage of whatever service is offered; any kind of training in this area is helpful.

Occasionally, employees are offered the option of taking cash instead of outplacement assistance. Depending on your economic situation, this may be a tempting offer. However, if you elect to take cash, be advised that it will be taxed. Outplacement benefits, on the other hand, are not taxable. In general, I recommend the outplacement option because, if you have selected the right firm and counselor, you will learn so much about yourself and have access to such good advice that the period that you are out of work may be significantly shortened. If you have made three or fewer job changes during your professional career, if it has been more than five years since you have conducted a job search, or if your separation from your past employer was extremely traumatic, you are particularly likely to benefit from outplacement services.

Once you have selected a service, be prepared to work hard at your job search. The outplacement firm is not paid to find a job for you. Rather, it is hired to train you in the most effective marketing strategies and to motivate you in spite of the rejection that inevitably occurs while you are looking for a job. You alone are responsible for getting a job. Take advantage of outplacement services, but do not try to defer your responsibility.

Appendix 5.1

Nationally Recognized Outplacement Firms

Cambridge Human Resource Group, Inc.
Two N. Riverside Plaza, Suite 2200
Chicago, IL 60606

Career Decision, Inc.
500 Park Boulevard, Suite 1245
Itasca, IL 60143

Drake Beam Morin, Inc.
100 Park Avenue
New York, NY 10017

Furst Transitions
One Tower Lane
Oakbrook Terrace Tower, Suite 640
Oak Brook Terrace, IL 60181

Jannotta, Bray & Associates
20 N. Wacker Drive, Suite 3600
Chicago, IL 60606

Lee Hecht Harrison
200 Park Avenue
New York, NY 10166

If you want more information, Kennedy Publications of Fitzwilliam, New Hampshire, publishes a directory of outplacement firms. You can order a copy of *Directory of Outplacement Firms 1993–1994* by calling (800) 531-0007 or (603) 585-6544. You can also contact the Association of Outplacement Consulting Firms in Parsippany, New Jersey, (201) 887-6667, to find out what consulting firms specializing in health care are available in your part of the country.

6

Dealing with Recruiters

An expert is someone who knows some of the worst mistakes that can be made in his subject and how to avoid them.

—Werner Heisenberg

Warning! I have written this chapter on recruitment because, at some point in your job search, you may be dealing with a search consultant. But I have grave reservations that you may have skipped my chapter on networking and turned right to this chapter, saying to yourself, "I don't need to network, I'll just get a search firm to find a job for me." This way of thinking is both inaccurate and dangerous. Search firms, for the most part, do not work for the individual, but rather for the employer. Although they may introduce you to more than one job opportunity, search consultants are not in the market to represent you. If you network properly, you will find out about all of the jobs available, including the ones the search firms are working on. Treat networking as your meat and potatoes, and the search firms as gravy. Network or not work. You are in charge of your job search.

With that caveat, I want to discuss two allies for all job candidates in health care administration—retained search firms and contingency search firms. They operate in two distinct fashions. Before deciding which type of firm to use, you must understand how they work. If you can appreciate the differences between firms, you will operate with more realistic expectations and actually wield greater control over the hiring process.

Executive search firms developed after World War II when an expanded economy caused shortages of skilled labor. A middle man or broker was needed to arrange employment. These early agencies often required the applicant to pay the fee. Today, such applicant-Paid-Fee (APF) firms are unheard of in health care and viewed as an anachronism in the search business.

The successors to the APFs were the contingency firms and the retained search firms. Contingency firms were paid the fee by the employer, but only if a hire was made. The fee was therefore "contingent" upon placement of the candidate. Retained search firms took a consulting approach to employment, focusing on the senior executive level. An executive search firm was engaged exclusively by an employer to seek candidates and a fee was paid during the course of the search—in other words, these firms were "retained."

Today both contingency and retained search firms continue to exist. On a dollar volume basis, they divide up the employment market fairly equally. In addition, search firms can be further subdivided. Some search firms have multispecialty offices, while others, such as our firm, offer industry-specific search consulting. There are thus four categories of search firms: specialized contingency, specialized retained, general contingency, and general retained. Whether a firm is specialized or multispecialty is a difference in degree, but whether a firm is retained or contingency is a difference in kind.

What are the differences between the retained search firms and contingency firms? Although the results of contingency and retained search are the same (someone gets hired), their approaches differ. Because these firms vary in both approach and fee payment, you must understand the differences and adjust your expectations and manner of dealing with them.

Retained Search Firms

The retained search process begins when the search consultant visits the client's organization for a site survey. During this phase, the consultant interviews the organization's executives to develop a candidate profile, the client's wish list. The consultant also secures information for prospective candidates such as community background, annual reports, and job description. In addition, the consultant establishes a compensation range for the position, plans the search schedule, sets target dates, and most importantly, gains a sense of the organization's dynamics and management style. Because of the amount of work that goes into this exhaustive and customized process, you can see why employers are usually very serious about filling a position when they engage a retained search firm.

After finding out just what the employer wants, the consultants identify qualified candidates by networking with potential candidates and centers of influence in the health care profession such as state hospital associations and graduate programs in health services administration. Through advertising and direct mail, consultants seek out executives to be candidates or to offer referrals to other executives. Retainer firms maintain extensive files; about 30 percent of the candidates come from those files. Having your resume on file with a search firm is a smart thing to do in your job search.

When you receive a call from a retained search consultant, you will hear a brief description about the opportunity as well as the specifications for the candidate, such as years of experience, educational background, and specific technical skills. If a strong match emerges between your background and the opportunity, the consultant will request your resume. He or she then checks references and verifies degrees and certifications.

If you seem particularly well suited for the position, the consultant will schedule an interview. During this initial screening process, the consultant is trying to produce three to five strong candidates who meet the client's needs. Expect to receive ongoing feedback on your standing in the search process. Be forthright about asking questions and generous in supplying information about yourself, including your special needs for making a move. Honesty and some healthy self-interest on your part will make sure that you are not wasting your time.

If you change your mind about the position and decide that you really do not want to actively pursue it, extend the courtesy of dropping out early. It is best for everyone involved: you, the client, the consultant, and the other candidates. If you coyly wait until the last minute to withdraw from this competitive process, you may not get a second chance with the retained search firm because valuable time has been spent on your candidacy.

Usually six to eight weeks into the engagement, assuming you and the consultant share a mutual interest in placing you in the position, the consultant will send candidate reports of you and the other finalists to the client, including references and interview notes.

The client will then decide to interview the finalists or request additional candidates. If you make it to this stage, you can now prepare for the interview confident that the position matches your goals and that going to the interview will be worth your time.

The retained search approach offers several advantages:

1. Before meeting the client personally, you are introduced through a comprehensive and objective information package. Your candidacy is given a fair chance, and even if the client decides on someone else, the consultant can offer you information, such as perceived weaknesses, that will only help you in future interviews.

2. If you are selected to interview with the client, the search consultant sticks with you through the process of the first and second interviews, community tours, and compensation negotiations.

3. If you are hired, a retained search firm also usually offers a one-year guarantee of your success. In other words, if you choose to leave or are terminated within a year, the search firm will conduct another search at no charge to the client. However cynical that may seem, it adds a boost to your move, because the client is assured of satisfaction.

4. Through retained search, you receive an expert recommendation for a high-level position, but preclude the chance of being presented for several positions at once or having a recruiter "campaign" for you. The endorsement and exclusivity of the retained search protects your credibility.

It is in your best interests to work with a number of retained search firms, keeping your file updated and establishing contacts over time. Be sure to be as selective as the firms are and narrow down your choices of acceptable positions, locations, and compensation. The consultant will wonder if you appear too eager for too many different types of positions. Even during those times when you are not actively looking for a new position, maintaining relationships with several retained search firms allows you to stay abreast of the career market and keep your options open.

When you send your resume to a retained search firm, be sure that you send a copy to the head of each office that the firm may have or to the individual who specializes in health care. As with other steps in your job search, such attention to detail speeds up the process. You will usually receive some sort of acknowledgment after you make the initial contact; however, it may be some time before you receive a promising response. Do not allow the elapsed time to discourage you. Keep in mind that retained firms work on fewer searches, so your activity with any one firm may be limited. But when activity does occur, it will usually be meaningful and substantial.

Contingency Firms

Contingency firms can give you lots of exposure and their approach usually works well for junior, middle-level, and unemployed executives. If you are a senior-level health care administrator, the contingency method can still work if the listing is legitimate and if it offers an excellent opportunity with an organization that you would not have contacted on your own. Contingency firms sometimes have "exclusives" with a client, but typically they do not. Therefore, be careful about granting them permission to use your resume.

Why the caginess about granting permission? And how do you go about handling this tricky matter? Many contingency firms have several offices nationwide. Your background may end up in a data base system that broadcasts your availability all over the country, which could be very positive or very negative, depending on your individual situation. Your resume might even end up on your boss's desk. Be sure you know where your resume is going. Be sure to define in writing the limits of your resume distribution.

Contingency search differs from retained search because the contingency firms do not have exclusive contracts with, or expenses paid by, the client. Under this system, site surveys, extensive candidate screening, and follow-through are uncommon. This approach is not less efficient or effective than a retained search; it is just different.

When a contingency firm calls you, you can expect a brief description without an exact identification of the position. The contingency recruiter needs to protect the listing from candidates who may try to approach the employer directly and from competing agencies.

Once the contingency recruiter has your resume, you will receive as much information as possible under the circumstances. You probably will need to research the employer on your own and evaluate whether your qualifications and aspirations fit the opportunity. Contingency recruiters tend to send your resume out to as many employers as possible.

The recruiter may want to help market your candidacy. Although this may produce numerous interview leads, invest your time judiciously and pursue only the strong opportunities. Contingency recruiters are enthusiastic advocates. It is your job to look after your interests and to avoid being cajoled into interviewing for a position that does not suit you. If you find a listing that interests you, keep in mind that you may be on your own during the interview process and the final negotiations.

Working with Recruiting Firms

To establish your expectations for a recruiter, ask the following questions:

1. Do you have an exclusive?
2. Can you provide complete information about the client?
3. Will you notify me before sending my resume to your client or any other clients?
4. Do you operate on a contingency fee or retainer basis?
5. What is your screening process—interviews, references, etc.?

Asking these questions will help you determine what kind of recruiter you are working with. You can then tailor your expectations and act accordingly.

Health care executives can easily confuse executive search firms of both types with outplacement/career counseling firms. Outplacement firms are in business to coach you on getting a job. For further information on outplacement, see chapter 5.

If you have not been exposed to executive search firms and want to know where to reach them, look in the classified sections of trade publications such as *Healthcare Executive*, *Modern Healthcare*, *Hospitals*, or *Health Week*. Another excellent source is the *Directory of Executive Search Consultants* from Executive Recruiting News (Kennedy Publications, Templeton Road, Fitzwilliam, New Hampshire 03447, (603) 585-6544 or (800) 531-0007. In addition, several respected retainer firms have been admitted to the American Association of Healthcare Consultants (AAHC), the only credentialing body for health care consultants. You can order AAHC's directory of firms by writing to them at 11208 Waples Mill Road, Suite 109, Fairfax, Virginia 22230, or by calling (703) 691-AAHC. Appendix 6.1 is a list of retained and contingency firms that specialize in health care.

When working with recruiters for both contingency and retained search firms, you need to be selective in the firms with which you work. You also need to be very clear about what you can expect them to do on your behalf. Do not hesitate to ask questions. You should keep in contact with the recruiters, but you want to strike a balance between calling too often and not calling enough. As with all your dealings during your job search, your interaction with recruiters should be yet another credit to your professionalism and integrity.

Appendix 6.1

Retained and Contingency Firms

Austin McGregor, International
P.O. Box 650398
Dallas, TX 75265

Barger & Sargeant, Inc.
22 Windermere Road
Suite H
P. O. Box 1420
Center Harbor, NH 03226-1420

Bill Bishop & Associates, Inc.
9511 Glenn Abbey Way
Jacksonville, FL 32256

Brissenden, McFarland,
    Wagoner & Fuccella
721 Route 202-206
Bridgewater, NJ 08807

The Cambridge Group
830 Post Road East
Westport, CT 06880

Carlson Associates
11444 West Olympic
    Boulevard, #1034
Los Angeles, CA 90064

M. L. Carter & Associates
P.O. Box 48148
Atlanta, GA 30362

Cejka & Company
222 South Central, Suite 400
St. Louis, MO 63105

CEMCO Medical
20 South Clark Street
Suite 610
Chicago, IL 60603

Chestnut Hill Partners
2345 Waukegan Road
Suite 165
Deerfield, IL 60015

Christenson & Hutchinson
466 Southern Boulevard
Chatham, NJ 07928

Robert Cole Associates, Inc.
1200 Westlake Avenue North
Suite 414
Seattle, WA 98109

Cole, Warren & Long, Inc.
2 Penn Center Plaza, Suite 1020
Philadelphia, PA 19102

Curl & Associates
707 Skokie Boulevard
 Suite 600
Northbrook, IL 60062

Provided by Career Decision, Inc., Itasca, Illinois.

Daudlin, DeBeaupre &
Company, Inc.
18530 Mack Avenue, Suite 315
Grosse Pointe Farms, MI 48236

Diversified Health Search
1 Commerce Square
2005 Market Street, Suite 3300
Philadelphia, PA 19103

Dick Dolan Associates, Inc.
125 West Orchard Street
Suite 100
Itasca, IL 60143

Eastman & Beaudine, Inc.
13355 Noel Road, Suite 1370
Dallas, TX 75240

Ed Edward Associates
184 Shuman Boulevard
Suite 200
Naperville, IL 60563

Fahey Associates
17 West 755 Butterfield Road
Oakbrook Terrace, IL 60181

Fiordalis & Associates, Inc.
600 Crown Oak Centre Drive
Longwood, FL 32750

Foley/Proctor Associates
89 Headquarters Plaza
North Tower, 14th Floor
Morristown, NJ 07960

Fortune Healthcare Group
2123 University Park Drive
Okemos, MI 48864

Fulton, Longshore & Associates,
Inc.
527 Plymouth Road, Suite 410
Plymouth Meeting, PA 19462

The Furst Group
P.O. Box 5863
Rockford, IL 61125

Garrett Associates, Inc.
P.O. Box 190189
Atlanta, GA 31119-0189

Gifford Associates, Inc.
625 North Michigan Avenue
Suite 500
Chicago, IL 60611

Guidry, East, Barnes & Bono
19506 Eastex Freeway, Suite 301
Humble, TX 77338

Hannahan Associates
2407 Ashland Avenue
Cincinnati, OH 45206

Healthcare Recruiters of
Michigan
30685 Barrington, Suite 175
Madison Heights, MI 48017

Health Industry Consultants, Inc.
9250 East Castilla Avenue
Suite 600
Englewood, CO 80112

Heidrick & Struggles, Inc.
125 South Wacker Drive
Suite 2800
Chicago, IL 60606

Hersher Associates
3000 Dundee Road, Suite 314
Northbrook, IL 60062

Higgins & Associates
108 Wilmot Road
Deerfield, IL 60015

Inteck Summit Group, Inc.
6540 Lusk Boulevard
Suite C-228
San Diego, CA 92121

Isaacson, Miller, Gilvar &
    Boulware
334 Boylston Street, Suite 500
Boston, MA 02116-3805

Ives & Associates, Inc.
400 East Town Street, Suite 210
Columbus, OH 43215

Robert William James Search
    Consultants
2360 North Broadway
Rochester, MN 59074
K.B.L.C. Associates
4203 Houghton Street
Philadelphia, PA 19128

A.T. Kearney, Inc.
1100 Abernathy Road
Suite 900
Atlanta, GA 30328-5603

The Kelly-Ashcroft Group
4250 Executive Square
Suite 440
La Jolla, CA 92037

King Associates
11545 West Bernardo Court
Suite 100
San Diego, CA 92128

Kittleman & Associates
303 South Wacker Drive
Suite 1710
Chicago, IL 60606

Korn/Ferry International
600 Montgomery Street
31st Floor
San Francisco, CA 94111

Lamalie Amrop International
1601 Elm Street
Suite 4246
Dallas, TX 75201

Langlois & Associates
P.O. Box 218
Accord, MA 02018

Lauer, Sbarbaro and
    Associates, Inc.
30 North LaSalle Street
Suite 4030
Chicago, IL 60602

R. E. Lowe Associates
8080 Ravines Edge Court
West Worthington, OH 43235

MAMSCO (Medical &
    Management
    Services Company)
244 Elm Road
Newbury Park, CA 91320

Management Science Associates
4801 Cliff Avenue
Independence, MO 64055

May Consulting Group
1127 Euclid Avenue
Statler Office Tower, Suite 375
Cleveland, OH 44115

McCormack & Farrow
695 Town Center Drive
Suite 660
Costa Mesa, CA 92626

McCracken, Wilcox & Bertoux
601 University, Suite 236
Sacramento, CA 95825

Medical Recruiters of America,
    Inc.
7771 West Oakland Park
    Boulevard, Suite 200
Fort Lauderdale, FL 33321
Miera Consultants International
4001 Indian School Road NE,
    #325
Albuquerque, NM 87110-3833

Bill Miller & Associates
P.O. Box 28308
San Diego, CA 92128

Ken Moon & Associates
4321 Reed Road
Arlington, OH 43220

Nast Associates, Inc.
P.O. Box 152385
Tampa, FL 33684-2385

NDI Services
42112 Crestview
Northville, MI 48167

Norman Broadbent
    International, Inc.
Sears Tower
Suite 9850
233 S. Wacker Drive
Chicago, IL 60606

Nutter Consulting Services
400 Albion Avenue
Suite 300
Cincinnati, OH 45246

P.A.R. Associates
27 State Street
Boston, MA 02109

Plemmons Associates
10520 Tuxford Drive
Alpharetta, GA 30202

Preston, Manthey &
    Associates
3433 Broadway Street NE
Suite 501
Minneapolis, MN 55413

Quigley Associates
345 83rd Street
Suite B
Burr Ridge, IL 60521

Paul R. Ray Company
301 Commerce Street
Suite 2300
Fort Worth, TX 76102

Roanoke Group
1701 West Northwest Highway
Grapevine, TX 76051

David Rowe & Associates, Inc.
515 West Maple Street
Hinsdale, IL 60521

Salick Healthcare
8201 Beverly Boulevard
Los Angeles, CA 90048-4520

Southern Medical Recruiters,
   Inc.
121 Del Mar
Corpus Christi, TX 78404

SpencerStuart & Associates
401 North Michigan Avenue
Suite 3400
Chicago, IL 60611-4244

Theken Associates
Route 66 Professional Center
P.O. Box 307
Randolph Center, VT 05061

Tyler & Company
1000 Abernathy Road
Suite 1400
Atlanta, GA 30328

Values Based Leadership
1716 South 153rd Avenue
   Circle
Omaha, NE 68144

Ward Howell International, Inc.
99 Park Avenue
New York, NY 10016

Weatherby Healthcare
25 Van Zant Street
Norwalk, CT 06855

Witt/Kieffer Ford Hadelman
   Lloyd
2015 Spring Road, Suite 510
Oak Brook, IL 60521

Zivic Group
611 Washington, Suite 2505
San Francisco, CA 94111

Part III

Securing Your Future

7

The Interview and Follow-Up

Carpe diem. (Seize the day!)
—Horace

This chapter is literally and figuratively the heart of this book and the key to guaranteeing that you will succeed in your job search. Although everything else in this book that precedes and follows this chapter will assist you, what I have come to learn from my work in health care recruitment is that the interview is the most important part of the job search. Individuals can be, and occasionally are, hired without resumes, without cover letters, without reference checks, and even without search firms, but never without an interview. Yet, it amazes me how many potential employees arrive at the interview unprepared, both physically and mentally. Preparation is essential for you as a candidate if you expect to come out ahead of other candidates who may match you in experience and ability. As the Scouts say, "Be prepared."

Mental Preparation for the Interview

Doing Your Homework

There are two equally important things you must know prior to the interview:

1. Know the organization and the hiring manager.
2. Know yourself.

Learn as much as you can about the job opportunity, the organization, and the hiring manager before the interview. As Roger Bacon said, *"Ipsa scientia potestas est."* ("Knowledge itself is power.") Mental preparation allows you to ask intelligent, forceful questions. There will be a marked contrast between the quality of the questions you ask and those asked by other candidates who did not prepare for the interview.

An acquaintance told me of going to a hospital for an interview for a position where the competition was extremely keen. On the way to the hospital, he made a detour by the state capital, where the hospital had recently submitted a certificate-of-need application that he was able to review in great detail. At the interview, he was in a position to ask insightful questions and to discuss intelligently the hospital's future plans. Needless to say, management was impressed by his level of preparedness, which showed his enthusiasm and his resourcefulness, and he got the job.

Information is readily available about organizations, if you just take the time to seek it. Doing your homework now will pay off in the long run. Magazines and trade publications can be valuable sources, as can annual reports of publicly held corporations. Government agencies often have extensive information that they are willing to share with the public. The data gathering may take some effort, but it will be well worth it.

Here are some methods you should consider when trying to get information on an organization:

- Have the human resources department send information when the inter-view is scheduled.
- Call the public relations department and ask for some hospital brochures.
- Call the local chamber of commerce and request a new-comer's package. Material on the hospital and its competition should be enclosed.
- See if the hospital has issued any bonds. Request an offering statement from your broker.
- Call the state hospital association and find out what information is available.
- Contact the state health planning agency to see if any CONs are currently in progress and to obtain any other pertinent information.

- Look up the hospital's statistics in the AHA guide.
- Read back copies of the local newspaper for information.

Here are some places where you can get information about the hiring manager:

- If he or she is a member of the American College of Health-care Executives, look up the individual's profile in the membership directory.
- Network with people who may have left the organization.
- Network with mutual acquaintances, such as vendors, consultants, and auditors.
- Make discreet inquiries with centers of influence such as association executives.
- Look up the person's profile in a bond offering statement.

Anticipating Questions, or Getting the Word

The second part of mental preparation for the interview involves anticipating what questions the interviewers will ask. If you can anticipate the questions, then you can be prepared with the answers. Many candidates, unfortunately and inexplicably, prefer to wing it on interviews. When the interview is over and they are thinking back on their answers, they often think, "Why did I say that? It was so stupid!" A properly thought-out and prepared answer would have allowed a better response and made a better impression. The following are some of the most frequently asked questions raised during interviews and some guidelines for your answers. Also, Appendix 7.1 is a comprehensive list of questions that our firm might ask of candidates. We call it "getting the word," and we give it to candidates so they can do their homework. The point is not to memorize and rehearse exact two-sentence replies, but rather to prime the pump, so that during the actual interview, you have a firm idea of what you want to include in your answers.

Guidelines to Frequently Asked Interview Questions

Tell me about yourself. This is the ultimate in open-ended questions and requires you to summarize your life. In general, you don't need to be overly specific. Stick with accomplishments, both personal and business, but gloss over negatives, such as divorce, job firings, and low periods in your life. Your answer should take less than 15 minutes. Otherwise, you are talking too much.

How would you describe your management style? Give a straightforward reply here: for example, "participatory," "situational," "team-oriented," "hands-on," or "mentoring." You might also include what types of people you like to work for.

Tell me about your experience. Include duties and specific accomplishments. It helps the interviewer to relate your experience to the opening if you can quote statistics such as budget figures, FTEs, and so forth.

Why did you leave that job? Your response needs to be carefully worded. Consider the difference between these answers: "I was fired," or "My supervisor and I began to have severe disagreements on the direction for my departments. After a period of trying to reconcile our differences, it became obvious to everyone that I should leave." Remember, your answer is subject to verification on a reference check, but you can put a positive spin on a termination.

Tell me about your strengths. Here is your opportunity to sell yourself. What is it that you do especially well? Now is *not* the time to be bashful—try to give three to five strengths.

What do you consider to be your weaknesses? Commonly called the suicide question, this one can open up a host of additional tricky questions if not answered properly. Here are some acceptable answers, followed by what could be called the corresponding weakness in parentheses:

- "I work too hard." ("I am a workaholic.")
- "I am too impatient for results." ("I lose my temper with incompetent people who don't meet my standards.")
- "I am too intent on accomplishing my goals." ("I lose sight of what is in the organization's best interests.")
- "I don't take enough time off." ("I am a loner, with no outside interests.")
- "I am persistent." ("I am stubborn.")

As you look at these examples and consider your own weaknesses, notice how important choosing the right word is when answering this suicide question. Mark Twain observed the importance of choosing your words carefully: "The difference between the almost right word and the right word is really a large matter—'tis the difference between the lightning bug and the lightning." The answers on the left shed a positive light on what, when phrased in the words in parentheses, could be construed as arrogance or a difficulty in getting along with co-workers. This is one question for which you really do want to frame an answer in advance.

One other thing—don't give an answer if it does not actually fit your character. Interviewers can usually tell if you are making something up. If you reply, for example, that you are too persistent, be ready to offer an example of when you doggedly worked at a tough problem.

You can also mention a *bona fide* weakness and add that you are working on it. For example, "I have joined Toastmasters to im-prove my public speaking, because that is an area where I have felt weak." Or, "I am finishing up a programming course that will strengthen my computer skills."

Another way to answer this question is by citing a strength taken to the extreme. For example, if you described yourself as a hard worker when asked to name a strength, then saying that you work too hard and occasionally neglect family relationships is an acceptable and plausible weakness. Note further that you are constantly trying to monitor the issue and balance work with family.

However you chose to address your weaknesses, navigate your way quickly and comfortably past this tricky question, and on to the next question. By all means, don't explore a weakness in any depth, or you may fall into a bottomless pit and be unable to climb out.

Avoid using the first person singular pronoun "I" as much as possible. Most organizations are not looking for the solitary knight who does everything alone. Organizations are looking for team players. "We" is the appropriate word to use when noting accomplishments.

How *Do* I Answer Those Illegal Questions?

Because of the Equal Employment Opportunity Commission's efforts to end discriminatory practices, certain questions are out of bounds. Unfortunately, you still may be asked a blatantly illegal question during an interview or in the first few weeks in a new position. However, in the interview setting when you want a position, you risk negative results if you challenge the interviewer on an out-of-bounds question.

One of the women whom I interviewed for this book was asked in an interview early in her career what kind of birth control she used. She had the luxury of a strong job market, walked out of the interview, and quickly found a position with another organization. She knew instantly that she would not want to work in an organization whose representatives lacked the professionalism and courtesy to steer clear of illegal questions. The likelihood of encountering such a question now, 20 years later, is much less, but you need to anticipate your reaction. If you are concerned about illegal questions, rehearse firm, diplomatic responses. You then can interview with any organization and avoid being blindsided.

I came up with some possible ways to extricate yourself from the illegal question dilemma:

1. "You know, my mother told me that you wouldn't have the nerve to ask me that question!"
2. "One of my friends told me she was asked a similar question, and she just chuckled and asked if it were a mock interview."
3. "I know you are kidding, so I'll go ahead to your next question."
4. "Is Diane Sawyer in the next room?"

These suggested responses show that I am a successful kidder. I am also a pretty good piano player, and I practiced, practiced, practiced to play well. To interview well, practice, practice, practice, especially on the tricky questions. Get to the point where you have a blithe, good-natured, yet rapid-fire response and you will make sure your performance during the interview avoids clumsy improvisation and sour notes.

My musical metaphor cannot hide the fact that answering illegal questions is serious business. Be ready. Your answer should reflect *your* personal style—the important thing is that you have a quick turnaround that keeps the interview going and the interviewer on the right track.

Physical Preparation for the Interview

Because of the power of first impressions, physical preparation for an interview is extremely important. You have only a short time to favorably impress the interviewer, so everything needs to be perfect. Follow this checklist:

1. *Arrive on time.* Obtain explicit directions from a knowledge-able hospital employee on exactly where the interview will be held. Leave time for traffic, parking, and acts of God. A few years ago, I was scheduled to speak at the University of Colorado in Denver. As usual, I left myself plenty of time, planning to arrive early. Unfortunately, my secretary had given me some garbled directions, which I was trying to decipher as I drove through downtown Denver. All of a sudden, I looked up and was in the middle of an intersection with cars flying at me from several directions. I careened the car into a curb, bursting two tires. Shaken but unhurt, I called the rental agency to pick up the car, flagged a cab, and walked into the auditorium on time. On another note, I once had a candidate interview with a client in Memphis. His instructions were to call the company upon his arrival and they would send a van. The van never came and he didn't call the company again for two hours. They were naturally unimpressed. Expect the unexpected and leave extra time. If you arrive early, use the time to mentally focus yourself for the interview.

2. *Look your best.* Women and men alike should wear conser-vative clothes. Men should wear a navy blue solid or pin-stripe suit, white or pale blue shirt, and a conservative tie. They should also get a haircut and trim their mustaches. Women should choose a suit in the classic colors of navy blue, taupe, or black. Hairstyles should also be classic. And all candidates should polish their shoes. Look sharp. I go on at length about professional dress in Chapter 10 if you want more specific recommendations.

3. *Be especially nice to secretaries.* Secretaries are often con-fidants of the boss. Treat them rudely and they may torpedo your candidacy. In fact, in some situations I have seen, the secretary casts the deciding vote when the hiring committee is voting on a candidate. Don't miss this chance to have someone speak highly of your courtesy. I once sat in on a search committee meeting where I was conducting the search for a major hospital system. Unbeknownst to me, the chair of the search committee had asked for feedback from the administrative secretary on how the candidates dealt with her when she was scheduling the first round of interviews. One

candidate was eliminated based on her negative comments. When the differences between the candidates are small, molehills become mountains.

4. *Don't smoke on an interview.* Smoking can indicate your nervousness and may also irritate the prospective employer. Even if the employer says its okay, or even smokes during the interview, refrain from smoking until the interview is over. Considering the growing trend toward smoke-free work-places, you don't want to identify yourself as a smoker, particularly in health care. (If you have enough motivation, now may be the best time to quit altogether, but that's another book.)

5. *Limit alcohol consumption.* The wartime slogan, "Loose lips sink ships," also applies to the interview process. Keep your faculties about you even in a party atmosphere. If lunch is a part of your interview, pass on a cocktail, so you are sharp in the afternoon. If you are invited to dinner, you might have a glass of wine.

6. *Check your handshake.* Is your grip strong and firm, or weak and fishy? Ask two friends for their opinion, and correct your handshake as necessary.

7. *Don't be glib.* Interviews are serious business. Don't relax because the interviewer is easygoing and "off the cuff." Stay on your toes.

Your Contribution to the Interview

It is extremely important to remember that an interview is a two-way street. As a candidate, you are expected to answer questions, but you should also ask questions. It is important, if you receive an offer, to make an informed decision. But you can only make an informed decision if you have adequate information, some of which the organization will freely offer, and some of which will not be volunteered. Therefore, ask as many questions as you can. The following are some questions you may want to ask:

1. Tell me about this organization.
2. Why is this position vacant? Is it newly created?

3. How many people have held the position in the last five years? Where are they working now?

4. If this is a new position, how will my success or failure be judged?

5. What method of performance appraisal do you use?

6. How is my supervisor viewed in the organization?

7. What is my supervisor's management style?

8. Whom do I supervise? What are their backgrounds, responsibilities, and so forth? What are they like? Ask for an organization chart if one has not been provided.

9. What is the hospital's competitive position?

10. What is the greatest challenge facing this organization?

Many candidates make the very common mistake of asking these questions of only one person and then assuming that the answer they receive is the correct or complete one. The answers to many of these questions will depend on the answerer's particular perspective, so you must direct the same questions to different people in the organization. There are certain questions that must be asked of everyone you meet in the organization. Inconsistent answers or hedging should serve as red flags for you, indicating potential trouble.

There is an exception to the rule of asking the same set of questions of several people. You should direct questions about salary to one person and one person only—the hiring manager. Only the hiring manager can answer these questions.

I am reminded of the time I was conducting a search for chief marketing officer of a large hospital. Knowing that the CEO had come up through the accounting ranks, I asked a question of the CEO in the presence of the executive team: "I guess, Jim, because you came up through the accounting ranks, then you must be a detail-oriented person. Should I look for someone who is comfortable giving you the level of detail you need?" Jim looked at me and said, "Larry, I'm not a detail person. I am a broad-brush executive, so that will not be an issue." As we left the table after lunch, the vice president of human resources pulled me aside and said, "Larry, I need to see you later." When later came, the vice president informed me that Jim was indeed a detail guy and that I had better get someone who could live with that fact. Did Jim lie to me? I don't think so. In Jim's view, he is much less detail-oriented than he was during his accountant days. In the vice president's view, compared with other CEOs he knew, Jim was very much concerned with details.

Because the interview is your first opportunity to come face to face with representatives of your future employer, you do yourself a disservice if you keep your questions to yourself. In your interview, you want to maintain objectivity and some skepticism about the organization to balance your eagerness to get the job. Make sure the position is one you will like and that will build your career. You owe it to yourself to keep high standards and to look out for yourself. Asking questions of the different people with whom you interview will equip you with the valuable, sometimes off-the-record, information you need if you want to work in the organization.

Even if you uncover a negative from your investigative questioning, or you think you don't want the job after all, conduct yourself during the entire interview as though you do. You need some distance to go over the data, and a demanding, stressful situation like an interview is not conducive to objective decision making. Keep a poker face and an open mind.

At the end of the interview, be sure to state your interest in the position and a desire to pursue further discussions. Ask what the next step will be and when they will plan to follow up with you on the results of your interview. Even if the interview has not gone well, maintain your zeal and energy until you are out of the building. You don't want to fade out of the room. Close the conversation with a strong handshake and a gracious acknowledgment for the interview.

One word of caution. Never accept a job on the spot. At least sleep on it for 24 hours. Think it through so that there are no loose ends. And be sure you get an offer in writing before you resign your current position. Then if a dispute arises later, you can refer to the written offer for resolution.

Interview Thank-You Notes

No matter how the interview went, common courtesy requires that you write a brief thank-you note and mail it within 24 hours after the interview. Do the following three things in your note:

1. Express thanks for the interview and the interviewer's time.

2. Restate your interest in the position.

3. Refer to future communication.

Depending on your own preference, you may either type or write the note longhand on good-quality business stationery. I personally prefer the handwritten note, particularly at the level of middle manager and above. Appendix 7.2 is an example of a thank-you note that could either be handwritten or typed. In either case, use the same care that you do in all your professional correspondence.

The Second Interview

There is a logical order to a job search. Step by step, from the strong lead to the acceptance of an offer, the job search is sequential and time-consuming. The seven steps should proceed in this order:

1. Lead
2. Cover letter and resume
3. Reference request
4. First Interview
5. Second Interview
6. Offer
7. Acceptance

You must let the process take its course. In this progression, each step lays the groundwork for the next. When building a house, you cannot build the second story before you complete the first one. Just as the resume focuses on getting the first interview, the first interview focuses on getting the second interview. Your goals for the first interview are the following:

- Make a good impression.
- Learn as much as you can.
- Get the second interview.

Your goals for the second interview are slightly different:

- Make a good impression.
- Clarify as much as you can.
- Involve your spouse.
- Get the offer.

Many guidelines outlined in this chapter are equally relevant for both the first and second interviews, depending on the interviewer's lead. In many respects, the second interview amplifies the first interview, by extending and broadening the investigation of both parties. However, there are some things to be aware of that set the second interview apart.

When you make it to the second interview, you are in the homestretch to obtaining an offer. From the starting pool of applicants that may have numbered in the hundreds, you have made it to the select few from which the employer chooses a finalist. Some people tend to relax and let down their guard at this point. Having gotten so close to their goal, they now feel that there is very little that they can do to influence the final decision and they are content to "let fate take its course." Do not place yourself in their number. In actuality, there is a great deal that you can do at this point to influence the decision-making process to your advantage. Your preparation for the second interview is critical to your success, so let's look at the areas that you need to cover in the second interview.

Questions generated in the first interview may remain unanswered. Perhaps you asked the same question on the first interview of several people and received inconsistent answers. Maybe you came up with additional questions when you were reviewing the first interview in your head. Regardless of their origin, you need to list all your questions in writing so that you can raise them in the second interview. It is really important to make sure that you have all your questions answered to avoid misunderstanding. As long as the list of questions is reasonable, you won't risk offending the hiring manager; limit yourself to no more than twenty questions. Likely areas of interest to you are benefits, the reporting structure and scope of authority, real estate issues, and spousal issues.

Questions about Benefits

You may have questions concerning benefits. In the first interview, you may have refrained from asking too many questions on this subject to avoid seeming money grubbing or security conscious. Because benefits vary greatly from organization to organization, you need the facts about benefits before you can weigh the job offer. Ask for the benefits handbook or any written form of the organization's benefits policy. Do not rely on the CEO or the hiring manager to have a complete and accurate grasp of the current benefits program. What is written in the benefits handbook takes precedence over anything that the hiring manager may promise in good faith. If there is any ambiguity, ask to meet with the appropriate human resources representative to get a more detailed explanation.

Questions about Reporting Structure and Scope of Authority

You may have discussed the reporting structure and scope of authority at length during the first interview. If so, just confirm what was said since it is possible that things may have changed and no one has updated you. If you did not discuss these questions at all in the first interview, then find out about the organizational structure and authority issues in depth during the second interview. If a current job description is available, go over it with the hiring manager. I know of one case where things got really screwed up. In 1993, the editor of a prestigious business journal thought he was hiring an individual to work under him as a senior editor. When contacted by another business publication, the new senior editor at the journal insisted that he was in charge and would be running the publication. This situation was an embarrassment to all concerned. It demonstrates the need to thoroughly cover the areas of reporting structure and authority.

Real Estate Issues

In preparation for the second interview, you should do your homework on your current house. Invite several real estate agents to come see your house and talk with you about the current real estate market. How hard will it be to sell it? What costs might you incur?

Has your contact at the hiring organization mentioned relocation costs? Will your prospective employer help out? Think about all these questions because you may be offered the job on the spot. If you are, you need to be ready to discuss these important real estate issues, which may bear directly on whether the offer is an attractive one.

Spousal Issues

Normally, when you are interviewing at the senior level, your spouse accompanies you on the second interview so that the prospective employer can get to know your spouse. In some organizations, the spouse is an integral part of the equation and is expected to interact with other spouses and executives in the company. In other firms, the spouse does not play a big role, and the firm only wants to know if he or she can interact comfortably with other executives and their spouses when called to do so. You may have already received a clue as to how important the spouse is in the organization, which will help prepare you and your spouse for the second interview. From the spouse's perspective, this opportunity is all important. Most likely, this will be the first time that he or she has a chance to meet the people with whom you might be working and to visit the new city. In addition, you may have questions relating to employment opportunities for your spouse or schools for your children. In fact, these issues are so crucial that they may require some work prior to the interview. If employment opportunities are important, arrange for your spouse to meet with someone who is knowledgeable in his or her field during the second interview period.

Ask for the Itinerary

Request the itinerary for the visit in advance, with the names, titles, and employers of the people whom you will be meeting. Even when applying for lower-level jobs, you typically will meet people within the organization. Interviewing at the senior level generally involves meeting with board members and, in some cases, prominent members of the community. Besides getting the word on whom you will meet on the second interview, having the itinerary ahead of time gives you the chance to plan some time to find out about housing and schools or to see people who are not at the interview.

The Social Side of the Second Interview

In most cases, second interviews include more social activities, so be ready to shift from business-related conversation to social conversation. Avoid the topics of religion, controversial current events, and politics. Ask lots of questions and listen attentively. One other tip: Find out about the social events ahead of time and the appropriate dress, and let your spouse know so you are both prepared.

Because the interview is so important to your success, you need to watch out for the little things that may make all the difference in the outcome. A bad haircut, an inappropriate remark, a misplaced fork, or a bad joke—any of these could take you out of the running for the position. Do not let your guard down. You have gotten so close to where you want to be. Don't blow it by doing something that you consider insignificant but that others might consider a real gaffe. At this part of the process, it is not your qualifications that are being scrutinized, but rather your personality. That may sound unfair, but your prospective employers want to be assured that your character and judgment suit their organization.

Testing

Now I will consider some relatively new developments in general employment practices that may or may not affect your interview process—psychological and drug testing. These ancillary elements are becoming increasingly widespread in the American employment market, and if you are beginning the job search for the first time in several years, you need to be aware of these new developments. Even if you have already taken some form of psychological test, you can use this chapter to learn more specific information and keep your perspective on these aspects of the job search.

Psychological Testing

If the phrase "psychological testing" makes you think of doctors in white lab coats carrying straitjackets, keep in mind what a colleague of mine, an organizational psychologist, has observed. He has administered tests to hundreds of people as part of the placement process and has noticed that some people do seem a little put off at the idea of having their personalities checked. More than once, however, at the end of the tests, people have said to him, "Hey, that wasn't half as bad as going to the dentist."

After the finalists for a position have been chosen, psychological testing can help identify the optimal person for that particular position. Obviously, you are not legally compelled to take a test, but you are strongly encouraged to graciously participate in the assessment. Remember that it is certainly in your own best interests to work in a position that is appropriate for you, that matches your own talents and personality. As an added benefit, you may learn more about yourself. If, for example, the tests show that you are extremely introverted, you may decide to work with a management psychologist on your own to help you to develop interpersonal skills.

The past decade has shown a marked increase in the use of psychological testing by executive search firms, hospitals, and other health care organizations. The incidence of testing increases with annual salary. The objectives is simple—to avoid turnover of high-level management and to avoid selecting the wrong person for the job. Hiring a person only to find out that the individual is not right for the job costs money, so the tests are administered to assess the fit between the candidate and the organization's needs. The tests are not an exercise in idle curiosity, but rather a management tool to increase the efficiency of the hiring process. Typically, a hospital or health care organization contacts an industrial psychologist who can conduct face-to-face interviews with the candidates and administer written psychological tests.

What can you expect? The complete assessment, interview and tests, usually lasts about four hours. Approximately one-third of the time is taken up by the interview, with the balance devoted to the written tests. During the face-to-face interview, the psychologist may ask about your goals, experiences, and personal background. The tests, which I discuss in detail below, seek to learn about you. Both components are trying to find out about you in reference to the particular position, *not to judge you.* You can be candid and relaxed, within reason. The employer is investing in this effort because you are a qualified, highly competent individual.

The exact composition of your tests depends on the needs for the position as determined by the psychologist. The field of industrial/organizational psychology allows for some variability concerning which tests to use. The information obtained from the tests can be organized in two different ways—inclusion or exclusion criteria. In other words, the client may specify some desirable characteristic that is a good indicator of success in the position or, conversely, may want to be alerted to any negative characteristic that would impede the candidate's performance.

Depending on what the client needs and how the psychologist wants to administer the tests, the psychological tests you may be asked to take can be of the following four categories:

- Aptitude tests
- Interest inventories
- Personality tests
- Honesty tests

Aptitude tests. Aptitude tests measure general aptitudes and should not be confused with an IQ test. Questions will test both your logical and verbal skills. You need not study for these tests, just do your best. You would not be in the running for the position if you were not a bright person, but the employer may want to know where your strengths lie.

Interest inventories. The so-called interest inventories measure your likes and dislikes. Obviously there are no right answers. One widely used test you may be asked to take is the Strong-Campbell Interest Inventory.

Personality tests. The many personality tests available attempt to systematically analyze a most complex thing—the human personality. We all differ one from another in subtle and not so subtle ways, so there can be no such thing as a perfect score. Be yourself and answer with candor. The tests include validity scales so you really cannot outwit them or make your personality seem different than it actually is. Common personality tests include the Meyers-Briggs Type Indicator, 16 Personality Factor Inventory (16 PF), Adjective Check List (ACL), California Personality Inventory, Self-Description Inventory (SDI), the Hogan Personality Inventory, and the Personal Profile, commonly known as the DISC.

Honesty or integrity testing. Honesty tests are very rarely used when hiring senior-level managers. Of all the tests, this category requires the most wariness on your part because of its very name. In any case, most psychological tests include validity scales to determine if the person is trying to change his or her response.

Appendix 7.3 lists short summaries of nine specific tests. If you care to, you can look over the tests' purposes, what the tests analyze, how long they take, and the number and type of test items. These tests are carefully designed and scrupulously administered. With many tests, the testing process itself is closely supervised by the American Psychological Association, which governs who can purchase and give the test. You can be reasonably confident that the person who administers the test is a licensed professional. Also, the examiner most likely is an outside consultant, retained by the hiring organization, who must meet the high ethical standards of his or her own professional association.

After you have completed the psychological evaluation, the psychologist will probably submit a written summary along with the scored tests to the organization. This evaluation becomes another piece of data in the hiring decision.

Drug Testing

Drug testing is no longer limited to professional athletes and transportation workers. Insurance companies routinely test customers, and some employers test job candidates. At this point, however, it is very unlikely that you will be asked to undergo drug testing. If you do, it is often disguised as a part of your physical, which may be administered by the organization's own medical team. An important point to remember is that since employment is a contractual relationship, prospective employers have the right to ask you to take a drug test as a condition of employment. Particularly in health care, determining that members of the workforce do not use illegal drugs is cost-effective and consistent with the goals of the organization.

This particular hoop may mark the low point of your job search, but it does not take much time or any special talent on your part. Since you might possibly jeopardize your chances of being considered for the position if you were to take offense, just take it in stride. Undergoing urinalysis gives the job seeker's slogan, "I will do *anything* to get this job," a whole new meaning.

Follow-Up

After the interviews end, and you enter the limbo of waiting to hear from the organization, you need to balance your presentation of yourself with your wish to find out whether you have the position. In your pursuit of the best possible position, you may struggle between indicating your interest and being too bold. Unfortunately, there is no simple answer to the right balance. It is one element of the job search that each candidate works out independently. If I had to err, I would err on the side of moderation.

Health care organizations tend to make hiring decisions slowly because many health care organizations are process oriented and many decisions involve gaining consensus. Because of scheduling problems, it may be hard to get people together to reach a consensus, but once a consensus is achieved, then the decision to hire will have the support of the people involved in the decision. Try to be as patient as you can. Nevertheless, if the decision to hire takes longer than four weeks, you may want to rethink whether you really want to work in a place that takes this long to make a decision.

When you telephone the interviewer or company contact, you must strike the right balance. Consider how you come across in your dealings with the interviewer as you follow up after the formal interviews have ended. Try to sound enthusiastic, not desperate; confident, not arrogant; persistent, not pushy. Obviously, you must use good judgment when deciding whether to call. Until you hear a "Sorry, but we are not interested," you still have the green light. Watch the signals, and proceed cautiously.

Just as asking the right questions during the interview itself helps your case, so does asking the right questions afterwards. A phone call every two weeks after the interviews is appropriate. Because the process moves slowly—on average, it takes 60 days from the day of the first interview to the day the offer is actually extended—calls more frequent than once every two weeks may actually hurt your candidacy. The following questions are permissible points you might raise during a telephone call after the interviews:

1. Do they need to schedule another interview?
2. What is going on with the company in general? Is downsizing, expansion, recrganization occurring?
3. How do hiring decisions dovetail with the calendar? Are they going to hold off on an offer until after the fiscal year begins?
4. How is the process coming?
5. Have they been able to contact your references?
6. What is the time frame? What in-house hurdles remain to be cleared before a decision is reached?

All these questions give you information, perhaps allay your anxiety over interminable delay, quell your eagerness to get an answer, and keep the conversation going.

Staying in Front of the Interviewer

By "staying in front of the interviewer," I do not mean stalking the hapless person in charge of the decision making, but rather implementing a low-key plan to maintain contact and visibility. Send an article on a topic that could prove useful to that person. When you telephone to check on the status of the decision making, state your availability and willingness to provide more information. You do not want to be a pest, but at the same time, you want the person to know you are thinking of the position and are alive and kicking.

Getting the Inside Scoop

The next step is tricky, but very productive. If at all possible, after you have interviewed, make an inside contact within the organization—perhaps someone you know professionally—who will be able to give you some helpful information. Even if your contact works in a different department than the open position, as an insider he or she can offer practical tips. For instance, the person might be able to tell you the best time to call—for example, early in the morning, after 5:00, late in the week. Your scout also might keep you up on any internal developments—an unexpected project or crisis that has pushed back the decision making. But be careful—you don't want to appear overeager or desperate.

Identifying the Decision Makers

When identifying the decision makers, as with this whole routine, you want to go far enough, but not too far. This step just increases your data bank. By knowing who makes the decisions about hiring for the position you want, you can make some reasonable assumptions about what kind of person the organization hopes to hire. In most cases, people hire people with whom they believe they can work well. Say, for example, that you find out the person actually deciding on the candidates began her career in materials management, like yourself. In this instance, you might have an edge that will buoy your confidence as you wait for the decision to be made.

Knowing who makes the hiring decisions does not give you license to directly contact them, especially if you are working with an intermediary. If the organization perceives that you cannot work within the process, you may be considered a renegade or a poor team player. In the world of hiring, there is an unwritten law of etiquette: Don't go around people. You may think the process in place wastes time, slows down decisions, or makes no sense, but there is a rationale behind the process.

By circumventing the proper channels, you risk many potential disasters.

1. You risk insulting the hiring manager.
2. You risk offending the board members, or whomever else you contact.
3. You risk seeming oblivious to how the game is played.

Just a clarification: The "proper channels" do not vary significantly when candidates are acting independently of retained or contingency firms. These guidelines apply to all candidates.

Elsewhere in this book, I endorse taking calculated risks, but directly contacting the behind-the-scenes decision makers is foolhardy. Going straight to the top works in Hollywood movies, but not in real life. At this point, you have done all you can.

Appendix 7.1

Structured Interview Format
(Prepared by the Staff of Tyler & Company)

I. Personal Background

    A. Tell me about your background.

    B. Where are you from?

    C. Outside interests?

    D. Academic achievements?

    E. What is your current financial situation? Any problems or litigation?

    F. How is your health?

II. Work Experience

    A. Tell me about your work experience.

    B. What were your duties?

    C. What did you like or dislike about each job?

    D. Specific achievements (list)?

    E. Why did you leave each job?

    F. What has been the biggest disappointment of your career?

III. Personality and Interpersonal Skills

    A. How would you describe yourself as others (subordinates) see you?

    B. Most important aspects of your life?

    C. How do you get along with people?

    D. What characteristics do you like in other people?

    E. What type of people rub you the wrong way?

    F. How do you react when someone criticizes your work?

    G. How do you handle interpersonal disagreements?

    H. Why did you choose this field of work?

    I. What do you consider to be your strengths? Weaknesses?

    J. Do you consider yourself organized? Creative? Disciplined? A hard worker? Why or why not?

    K. What causes stress for you? How do you handle it?

IV. Supervision and Management Style

    A. Describe your management (or your selling, planning, etc.) style.

B. What are the two most important points or considerations to remember when managing, dealing with, or handling people?

C. Characteristics a good supervisor should have?

D. How could your last supervisor have been better?

E. How would you describe your relationship with other departments? Review by department.

F. What financial reports must you generate that help you to manage your department?

G. When faced with a difficult management problem, whom do you consult for a resolution of the problem?

H. Rate yourself in the following areas: Planning? Organizing? Controlling? Motivating?

V. Job Expectations

A. Why are you leaving your present job?
   1. What are its drawbacks?
   2. Does your supervisor know you are looking for a change?

B. What are you looking for in a job?
   1. Ideal job?
   2. Future goals?

C. What appeals to you about our position?

D. What can you do for us?

E. Current salary?

F. Salary requirements?

G. Time frame for making a change?

H. Are you considering other job opportunities?

I. Geographical preference?

J. Have you discussed relocation with your family members? What was their response?

K. Does your spouse work? What profession?

Appendix 7.2

Example of a Thank You Note

February 15, 1994

Mr. Bob Mullins
Executive Director
Holy Redeemer Hospital
9200 Monte Verde Boulevard
Houston, Texas 77135

Dear Bob:

Thank you for taking the time to meet with me yesterday. You run a top-drawer operation and I would welcome the chance to become a part of your future growth as the Director of Support Services at Holy Redeemer.

I look forward to hearing from you soon. Again, thank you for your consideration.

Sincerely yours,

Stephen Grumbacher

Appendix 7.3

Descriptions of Some Commonly Administered Psychological Tests

Strong-Campbell Interest Inventory

This multiple choice test asks the examinee to respond "like," "indifferent," or "dislike" to 325 items covering a wide range of occupational tasks. Topics include occupations, school subjects, activities, leisure activities, and types of people.

Meyers-Briggs Type Indicator

This test, consisting of 126 to 166 items, measures four bipolar personality aspects: introversion/extroversion, sensing/intuition, thinking/ feeling, and judging/perception.

The World of Work Inventory

This 518-item test has two parts: (1) 98 multiple choice items testing various aptitudes (abstractions, spatial form, verbal, mechanical, electrical, and clerical) and (2) 420 items assessing 12 job-related temperament factors.

California Personality Inventory

This test has 480 items measuring 18 socially desirable behavioral tendencies: dominance, capacity for status, sociability, social presence, self-acceptance, sense of well-being, responsibility, socialization, self-control, tolerance, good impression, communality, achievement via conformance, achievement via independence, intellectual efficiency, psychological mindedness, flexibility, and femininity.

Self-Description Inventory (SDI)

This test consists of 200 items assessing eleven personal description and six vocational scales. The personal scales are cautious/adventurous, nonscientific/analytical, tense/relaxed, insecure/confident, conventional/imaginative, impatient/patient, unconcerned/altruistic, reserved/outgoing, soft-spoken/forceful, lackadaisical/industrious, and unorganized/orderly. The vocational scales are realistic, investigative, artistic, social, enterprising, and conventional.

Adjective Check List (ACL)

This test uses verbal responses to assess personality. It is frequently used by human resources professionals when interviewing job candidates.

Hogan Personality Inventory

This 300-item true and false test measures six traits: intellect, adjustment, prudence, ambition, sociability, and likability. It also includes six occupational scales: service orientation, clerical performance, sales performance, management performance, stress tolerance, and reliability.

16 Personality Factor Inventory (16 PF)

This general personality inventory appears in several forms of varying lengths. The test is widely used by organizational and industrial psychologists specializing in employment. It assesses self-discipline, stability, extroversion, assertiveness, and ability to work.

Personal Profile (DISC)

This quick (takes less than ten minutes) test identifies any of four behavior types: Dominance, Influencing, Steadiness, and Cautiousness. The Personal Profile is based on the DISC model of behavior developed by William Moulton Marston and John Geier. It generates a lengthy report on the individual's behavior, including suggestions and strategies for more effective behavior. We use it at Tyler & Company both in-house and in our work with job candidates.

8

Evaluating Job Offers and Employment Contracts

He who seizes the right moment, Is the right man.
—Goethe

Congratulations! You have just received a job offer, which is what you have been directing all your energy toward for the past several months. So why do you feel uneasy? The decision whether or not to accept the offer and make the move can drive you and your family crazy. It is difficult comparing your old job with the new one. The salary itself is higher, but moving will cost money; the benefit package sounds equal, but you are not positive. And will it be a smart move for your career? You have good reason to feel uncertain. Deciding to change jobs is one of the most important and difficult decisions you can make.

Factors to Consider in Evaluating Job Offers

There are many factors involved in making the decision to change jobs, and candidates often have trouble determining which factors are most important. Because changing jobs is not a routine matter, our own experience is usually not adequate to help differentiate between relevant job factors and the incidental ones. Let me assure you that there are only three important considerations: money, opportunity, and location.

Money

It is only natural that money should be a consideration as you evaluate a job offer. We are all money-oriented to varying degrees, and money is the denominator for keeping score on how successful we are in our careers. "Money" really means total compensation: salary, bonus, benefits, deferred compensation, and other related items. As you evaluate a career decision, you must weigh in your mind the compensatory advantages of the offer. There should be a substantial monetary reason for making the change. Most candidates will not consider a move for less than a 15 percent increase, assuming all other things are equal. (Of course, all other things are seldom equal.) Evaluating the monetary factor is the most straightforward of the three because money is easily quantified, and thus easily compared to present compensation or other offers.

As you evaluate compensation, consider the total package. An offer of $80,000 plus a potential bonus of up to $15,000 is probably more attractive than a salary of $85,000. A car, club memberships, and other fringe benefits sweeten the deal. And don't forget to check on state and local income and property taxes at the new location. Many candidates discover too late the monetary effect of moving from a low-tax area to a higher one. State income taxes are deductible on the federal tax return, so the bottom line effect is less than the actual state tax, but you still want that bottom line to warrant the move.

Most compensation offers are negotiable, although the specific salary may not be. If the salary offer is unacceptable, you have several alternatives. The first and most obvious one is to negotiate a higher starting salary, perhaps by producing salary surveys indicating the earnings of individuals with your level of experience. If this approach fails, try another tactic. Negotiate for a signing bonus or a moving expense allowance considerably higher than your actual moving expenses. Or you could accept the position with the provision that you will be guaranteed the salary you seek after a six-month review. If all else fails, accept the position like this: "John (the boss), I am ready to go to work for Memorial Hospital. I accept the position right now if you can get the salary to $_____." This approach gives John the chance to push for the salary change. You have taken away the uncertainty of turning down his offer and given him the ammunition to clear the path for your contract signing.

Money is only one of the three factors to consider. Curiously enough, surveys consistently show that money is far down on the list of what people actually want from their jobs, below the challenge, the type of people one works with, and the type of work performed. If so, why do people expect significant salary increases for changing jobs?

The salary increase compensates them for the risk and exposure associated with the job change. As a general rule, the higher the risk and responsibility, the greater the increase. If a situation is risky, don't sell yourself short on salary. Remember also, if a job is extraordinarily risky, you should negotiate a severance package.

Opportunity

What is opportunity? Different individuals have different definitions, but in general, opportunity means a chance to expand the scope of your responsibilities, duties, or span of control. Opportunity may also mean a chance for unlimited growth in the long term, a chance to get away from a repressive management style, or a chance to run things your own way. It can also be defined in terms of challenge, the type of work, and the type of people with whom you work. In any case, the precise definition of opportunity is purely subjective. It depends on your own personal view of short-term and long-term career goals. Therefore, only you can decide what is a "real opportunity."

We have observed in our search practice that many people view opportunity as a new and exciting challenge. Many health care executives have an ongoing desire to improve on their experience and are willing to leave a secure and satisfying position just for the challenge of doing something different, and usually harder. Like those who climb Mount Everest, many individuals seek out a new challenge just because it is there.

If you are eager to pursue a new professional challenge that you deem an opportunity, be as deliberate and thorough as a mountain climber before you begin. Get the facts. Talk to people other than the ones to whom you have been introduced in the organization. Outsiders who have dealings with the facility or company can be helpful in characterizing its strengths, weaknesses, management style, or viability. If you can, talk to people who have left the organization; they are excellent sources of scuttlebutt. During your interview, listen for the names of people who have left and where they now work, so that you can call them. Find out all you can about the position itself and its history. If the position is newly created, what are the performance criteria? If the position has existed for a long time, how long has it been vacant? Who has been covering the responsibilities? Why is it vacant? How many people have held the job in the last ten years? Where are they now?

Additionally, in order to determine if the position is really an opportunity, you need to determine your prospects in the organization. Ask about your career path. Such questions should be addressed in the first interview and should be asked of more company personnel than just the hiring manager. Some hiring managers will not intentionally lie, but in their eagerness to attract a strong candidate, will paint a rosier picture than actually exists. In order for you to have a realistic picture of the position, you must ask the same set of questions of each person with whom you interview. Inconsistencies in the answers should be a red flag that you may want to pass on this opportunity.

Of the three factors in evaluating job offers, opportunity is the hardest to gauge. In the final analysis, it boils down to "you pay your money and you take your chances." Your gut instincts may be your best judge, provided you have asked the right questions. If your gut tells you something doesn't feel right, keep asking questions!

Location

In my opinion, location is the single most important factor in job change for senior executives. That may be because I live in Atlanta, a city whose beauty, lifestyle, and friendliness make it very attractive; I constantly hear the same view from others, who will say, "Keep your eyes open for me. I don't want to leave Atlanta." Of course, there are many great places to live in the United States, and most exec-utives will give up a lot in order to live where they are happy. Location is important not only for recreational purposes after the workday ends, but also for the well-being of your family.

A common mistake when evaluating location is to reject a position out-of-hand without ever making a site visit. For example, someone who considers Atlanta to be an acceptable location, while casually dismissing Birmingham, Nashville, or Charlotte, is foolhardy, unless the candidate has visited those cities numerous times. Many candidates close the door on certain locations because of preconceived notions. Pittsburgh, for example, received bad press back in the 1950s, but today it is highly regarded for its quality of life and has excellent opportunities in health care administration. You should remain flexible within a general region (such as the Southeast) and population size (such as 100,000) and fill in the particulars after the site visit. In evaluating location, consider the general economic conditions of an area, demographic trends, quality of the school system, how you fit into the community, and the types of cultural activities.

Location is also the factor upon which a spouse exerts the greatest influence. My area of expertise is not marital relations, dual-career marriages, or the effect of corporate life on a family, but I can offer a few guidelines from my experience working with candidates:

1. *Involve your spouse in the job change decision from the very beginning.* If you have not communicated well in the last few years, the disruption of a job change could lead to a divorce. If you involve the other person, the job change may actually strengthen your relationship.

2. *If you are part of a dual-career marriage, one of you will have to compromise.* In dual-career marriages, one of you may have to sacrifice this time, and the other may sacrifice the next. The problems encountered by dual-career marriages in making job changes are geometric, not arithmetic.

3. *When it comes to location, the whole family's opinion should be weighed heavily.* Your children's lives will also be affected, so involve them in the process. After you and your spouse gather information and impressions from the site visit, make sure you discuss the proposed relocation as a family. You all may be pleasantly surprised with the new location.

Additional Factors

In addition to money, opportunity, and location, candidates sometimes consider the following lesser factors:

- *Retirement plan.* Look for vesting scales only if you are required to contribute. I recommend that you establish an IRA for yourself because you will probably move again.

- *Dental insurance.* If your family includes potential customers for the orthodontist, dental insurance might seem important. Include it in the evaluation of money.

- *Relocation and expenses of selling your house.* Consider under the money factor. Your new employer may be very cooperative.

- *Need to be close to relatives.* Realistically you have to be willing to relocate to advance in the health care field.
- *Private school for the children.* Evaluate as part of location.
- *Travel requirement.* If you are considering a job requiring a lot of travel, consider these thoughts:

  1. If the company says the job requires 50 percent travel, ask how this percentage is calculated. Does it mean that out of seven nights a week, you are on the road for four of them? Or that half of the staff is in town 100 percent of the time and the other half travels 100 percent of the time? Or does it mean that you are gone 50 percent of the time on day trips and can sleep in your own bed at night?
  2. Verify the information with others who have had the job.
  3. Investigate how the company treats travelers. Can you keep the frequent flier mileage or must you give it up? Are you on a low per diem? Do you have to travel Sunday night or can you take an early flight on Monday morning?
  4. Does your spouse accept the amount of traveling you have to do? Is he or she independent enough so that the travel will not be a problem?

  If you have never traveled extensively in your work, talk with some friends who have. Most heavy business travelers, myself included, don't really like travel, but we tolerate it well.

Common Mistakes

The most common mistake when evaluating job offers is failing to focus on the three key factors. The second most common mistake is "backing into a job"—acting out of negative motivation or desperation. People are most likely to make this mistake when they are extremely dissatisfied in their present jobs, when they are about to be terminated, or when they have been unable to find work. In trying to get out of a tough situation, candidates sometimes take the first job that comes along. For example, one candidate I know had worked for a "screamer." His primary criterion in finding a new position was to work for an organization that had fairly calm management. Where does his reasoning fit within the three criteria? It doesn't. By concentrating on the three important factors, he came to realize that eliminating the screamer was not a sound basis for selecting a new job.

Love 'Em or Leave 'Em

I find in my practice that if at least two of the three factors are judged by the candidate as positive, then the candidate will probably accept the offer from the client company. My advice reflects that observation. If you find that two of the three factors are very positive, then accepting the position will probably be a good move. If only one factor is positive, pass and work toward getting a different, presumably better offer. If all three factors are positive, jump at the opportunity.

If you are having trouble making the decision, you probably need more information in the area where you are having problems. For example, if you are evaluating the money factor and trying to decide about the selling price of your house, invite some realtors to get a realistic idea of what price you can expect. If there is a good deal of uncertainty in other areas, contact an objective third party and discuss the proposed job change. If you are fortunate enough to have a mentor, now is the time to call on that person and consult the wisdom of an informed outsider. Changing jobs and developing your career can be fun and exciting, or it can be draining and painful. The combination of knowledge and confidence will only strengthen your bargaining power and obtain optimal results. As you make your decision, remember the three factors: money, opportunity, and location. I am confident that you will then minimize the uncertainty surrounding job offers and know when to love 'em or leave 'em.

Employment Contracts

Today we operate with a revised employment-at-will doctrine, and therefore you and your employer can establish conditions of employment. In health care administration, job termination goes with the territory, and you may need to negotiate a formal employment contract to protect your interests. The trend in the last five years has been toward using employment contracts, which mirrors the trend in other businesses. Nearly 50 percent of hospital CEOs now have some type of contract, according to the American Hospital Association. Typically, only top executives sign formal employment contracts.

Should you broach the possibility of using a contract with your prospective employer, and if so, at what point in the negotiation? As soon as you have been offered the position, you can suggest using a formal employment contract as one of your conditions of employment. Hospital boards are more familiar with them than they were in the past and, in fact, may introduce the topic as a part of the job offer if they believe that you expect it.

Realistically, you should be reasonable in the areas covered by the contract. You must balance your interests against what the market will bear. To understand the use of employment contracts, review any actual contracts that you can get your hands on—it only takes a little creativity. One resource is *Contracts for Healthcare Executives*, published in 1987 by the American College of Healthcare Executives, which discusses the issues of employment contracts for health care administrators and provides sample documents. Appendix 8.1 is a copy of the employment contract used by Tyler & Company for hospital chief executive officers. I offer it for discussion purposes only, in order to illustrate what an employment contract may actually address.

In recent years, the balance of power in the terms of employment contracts has shifted from the executive to the health care organization, reflecting the law of supply and demand in a crowded market. But truly exceptional candidates can still request and receive a contract. Both parties have rights, and a thorough and clearly worded contract may be the best way to protect them.

Terms of the Contract

Likely issues to include in an employment contract include the following:

- *Expected duties*. Specify in complete detail.
- *Compensation*. Includes benefits, salary, and increasingly, incentive pay.
- *Dispute resolution*. Specify which state laws will apply and which methods will be used to settle problems.
- *Basis for termination*. List the circumstances under which you can be terminated.
- *Noncompete agreement*. Should be reasonable, in terms of distance, duration, and type of work.
- *Sick leave*. Indicate company policy.
- *Maternity leave*. Should be as clear as possible.
- *Severance*. Should be a reasonable length of time, 1–2 years. Includes continuation of health and life insurance.

- *Insurance coverage.* Specify level and cost to you.
- *Ownership of work product.* Your employer has a right to expect this.
- *Illegal activity.* Define and spell out consequences.

An enforceable employment contract must have reasonable objectives. If there is fraud or deception, or if the offer or its acceptance was made under pressure, it probably won't hold up in court. You cannot be required to do anything illegal, unethical, or discriminatory.

You may be asking yourself if you should consult an attorney. In my opinion, you should. You need expert legal advice to know exactly what you are agreeing to. Also, because labor laws vary so much from one state to another, you will better protect yourself by consulting with an attorney familiar with employment issues in that particular state.

Related Contracts

You may well be asked to sign a confidentiality or nondisclosure agreement. It will cover the following:

- A promise not to disclose confidential information
- A transfer of liability from the company to the employee if the employee speaks out of turn

Less Formal Contracts

It is possible that you may not have an employment contract. Your employer may simply ask you to sign and return the hiring letter. In that case, make a copy of the letter and treat it with the same respect with which you treat a contract. Or you may verbally contract to begin work, literally on a handshake. When you accept the organization policy guidelines, personnel manual, or company handbook, you are agreeing to the conditions for employment. Know what they are. Read the contents thoroughly, as soon as you possibly can.

The Three R's of Employment Contracts

As an employee entering into a contract with an employer, you must know your *rights*, your *responsibilities*, and your *recourse* to breach of contract or discrimination. Employment contracts are legal documents. Don't sign one unless you understand it.

Breach of Contract

If your employer breaches the employment contract, you can negotiate, mediate, or sue for damages. But the contract goes both ways; you must uphold your part of the bargain. The best employment contract protects both you and the employer, balancing your interests with those of the organization. The most common response to a breach of employment contract is seeking money to compensate for loss caused by the breach. The amount of damages should be reasonable.

Finally, make sure you already have a job before you sue a former employer. Suing your employer, no matter how justified, is looked upon unfavorably by prospective employers. Don't allow pursuing legal action to become a full-time job.

Further Reading

Bequai, August. *Every Manager's Legal Guide to Hiring* (Homewood, Illinois: Dow Jones, Irwin, 1990).

Eubanks, Paula. "Boards, Execs More Savvy about CEO Contracts." *Hospitals* (February 1990).

Milko, George, Kay Ostberg, and Theresa Meehan Rudy. *Everyday Contracts: Protecting Your Rights* (New York: Random House, 1991).

Reese, Jennifer. "More Up-Front Severance Deals." *Fortune* (June 3, 1991).

Rowland, Mary. "Negotiating an Employment Contract." *Working Woman* (February 1990).

Appendix 8.1

Tyler & Company Recommended Employment Contract for Hospital Chief Executive Officers (Draft for Discussion Purposes Only)

> This contract has been derived from the model contract recommended by the American College of Healthcare Executives with additions based upon the practical experience of the staff of Tyler & Company.
>
> Employment contracts are legal documents and as such should be prepared by an attorney. This document is merely a basis of knowledge and discussion for board members and the CEO. Paragraphs denoted by asterisks (*) may be limited by state law. Consult your attorney for final document preparation.

This agreement, made and effective as of the ___day of _____, 19_____, between _____ of _____, a nonprofit corporation and _____of_____.
WHEREAS, _____, desires to secure the services of _____ for _____ years from the effective date of this contract and _____ desires to accept such employment.

NOW, THEREFORE, in consideration of the material advantages accruing to the two parties and the mutual covenants herein, _____ (hereafter called the Hospital), and _____ (hereafter called _____), agree with each other as follows:

1. _____ will render full-time professional services to the Hospital in the capacity of Chief Executive Officer of the Hospital for the _____ year term of this contract. He/she will at all times, faithfully, industriously and to the best of his/her ability, perform all duties that may be required of him/her by virtue of his/her position as Chief Executive Officer

and all duties set forth in Hospital bylaws and in policy statements of the Board of _____.
It is understood that these duties shall be substantially the same as those of a chief executive officer of a business corporation.

_____ is hereby vested with authority to act on behalf of the Board in keeping with policies adopted by the Board, as amended from time to time. In addition, he/she shall perform in the same manner any special duties assigned or delegated to him/her by the Board.

2. a) In consideration for these services as Chief Executive Officer, the Hospital agrees to pay _____
   a salary of $_____ per annum or such higher figure as shall be agreed upon at an annual review of his/her compensation by the Board. This annual review shall occur three months prior to the end of each year of the contract for the express purpose of considering increments. The salary of $_____ shall be payable in equal monthly installments throughout the contract year. _____
   _____ may elect, by proper notice given to the Hospital prior to the commencement of any calendar year, to defer such portion of said salary for such year to such date as he/she may designate in such notice of election, such deferred amounts to be credited with periodic interest in accordance with policies established by the Hospital.

   b) An annual performance review shall provide the Chief Executive Officer with specific information on performance in the critical areas of hospital administration. The performance review will be conducted by the Executive Committee or a specifically designated group of Board members and will include
   • feedback on specific performance criteria for the current period,
   • developmental actions to enhance performance, and
   • establishing mutually agreed upon objectives to be accomplished during the subsequent performance period.

3. a) _____ shall be entitled to _____ weeks of compensated vacation time in each of

the contract years, to be taken at times mutually agreed upon by him/her and the Chairman of the Board.

b) He/she shall also be entitled to ___ weeks of compensated sick leave in each contract year, to be taken if required, throughout the contract year.

c) In the event of a single period of prolonged inability to work due to the results of sickness or an injury, _____ _____ will be compensated at his/her full rate of pay for at least ___ months from the date of the sickness or injury.

d) In addition, _____ will be permitted to be absent from the Hospital during working days to attend professional meetings and to attend to such outside professional duties in the hospital field as have been mutually agreed upon between him/her and the Chairman of the Board. Attendance at such approved meetings and accomplishment of approved professional duties shall be fully compensated service time and shall not be considered vacation time. The Hospital shall reimburse_____ _____ for all expenses incurred by him/her and his/her spouse incident to attendance at approved professional meetings, such entertainment expenses incurred by _____ in furtherance of the Hospital's interests, provided, however, that such reimbursement is approved by the Chairman of the Board.

e) In addition, _____ shall be entitled to all other fringe benefits to which all other employees of the Hospital are entitled.

4. The Hospital agrees to pay dues to professional organizations and societies and to such service organizations and clubs of which _____ is a member, approved by the Chairman of the Board as being in the best interests of the Hospital.

5. The Hospital also agrees:
   a) to insure _____ under its general liability insurance policy for all acts done by him/her in good faith as Chief Executive Officer throughout the term of this contract;

   b) to provide, throughout the term of this contract, a group life
      insurance policy for _____ in an
      amount equivalent to $50,000 plus three times his/her sal-
      ary, payable to the beneficiary of his/her choice;
   c) to provide comprehensive health and major medical insur-
      ance for _____ and his/her family;
   d) to purchase travel accident insurance covering _____
      _____ in the sum of $150,000;
   e) to furnish, for the use of _____, an
      automobile, leased or purchased at the beginning of alter-
      nate fiscal years, and reimburse him/her for expenses of its
      operations;
   f) to contribute on behalf of _____ to
      a retirement plan qualified under the Internal Revenue Code,
      at the rate of $_____ per month.

6. The Board may, in its discretion, terminate _____
   _____'s duties as Chief Executive Officer. Such
   action shall require a majority vote of the entire board and
   become effective upon written notice to _____
   _____ or at such later date as may be specified in
   said notice. After such termination, all rights, duties and obligations of both parties shall cease except that the Hospital shall
   continue to pay _____ his/her
   monthly salary for the month in which his/her duties were
   terminated and for twenty-four consecutive months thereafter as
   an agreed upon termination payment. Such pay shall be made in
   all instances except in the event of intentional illegal conduct on
   the part of the Chief Executive Officer. During this period,
   _____ shall not be required to per-
   form any of the duties for the Hospital or come to the Hospital.
   Neither shall the fact that he/she seeks, accepts and undertakes
   other employment during this period affect such payments.
   Also, for the period during which such payments
   are being made, the Hospital agrees to keep _____
   _____'s group life, health and major medical in-
   surance coverage paid up. He/she shall be entitled to
   outplacement services offered by the Hospital.

7. Should the Board in its discretion change _____
_____'s duties or authority so it can reasonably be found that he/she is no longer performing as the Chief Executive Officer of the Hospital, _____
_____ shall have the right, in his/her complete discretion, to terminate this contract by written notice delivered to the Chairman of the Board. After such termination, _____
_____ shall be entitled to the termination payment described in Paragraph 6, in accordance with the same terms of that Paragraph.

8. Should _____ in his/her discretion elect to terminate this contract for any other reason than as stated in Paragraph 7, he/she shall give the Board 90 days written notice of his/her decision to terminate. At the end of 90 days, all rights, duties and obligations of both parties to the contract shall cease.

9. Negotiations for the extension of this contract, or for an agreement on the terms of a new contract, shall be completed, or the decision not to negotiate a new contract shall be made, not later than the end of the tenth month of the final contract year. By mutual agreement of the parties, this contract and all its terms and conditions may be extended from year to year or for a term beyond its initial term by a simple letter exchanged between the parties, at any time during the contract term.

10. Confidentiality. Employee agrees to keep confidential and not to use or disclose to others during the term and for so long thereafter as such information remains confidential, except as expressly consented to in writing by the Hospital or required by law, any secrets or confidential medical, personnel, technological, or proprietary information, patient information, or trade secrets of the Employer or any matter or thing ascertained by Employee through Employee's association with Employer, the use or disclosure of which matter or thing might reasonably be construed to be contrary to law or against the best interests of Employer. Employee further agrees that should Employee leave the active service of Employer, Employee shall neither take nor

retain, without prior written authorization from Employer, any papers, medical data, patient lists, patient records, files or other documents (or copies thereof) or other confidential information of any kind belonging to Employer pertaining to the business, sales, financial condition, products, patients, professional or medical activities, or other activities of Employer.

*11. Offers to Hospital Employees. Recognizing (i) the special nature of the relationship existing, or which will exist, between Employee and the other personnel that Employer employs or retains and (ii) that the recruiting and training of personnel by Employer is a costly and time-consuming endeavor, Employee agrees that Employee shall not, during the Term, and for a period of two (2) years thereafter, directly or indirectly, through any manner or means, impair or initiate any attempt to impair the relationship that exists between Employer and personnel employed or retained by Employer, through offers of employment or offers of contracts for services to be rendered by such personnel or otherwise.

*12. Non-Competition Agreement. Employee recognizes that Employer's entering into this agreement is induced primarily because of the covenants and assurance made by Employee herein, that Employee's covenant not to compete is necessary to ensure the continuation of the business of Employer, and that irrevocable harm and damage will be done to Employer in the event that Employee competes with Employer within the area described below. Therefore, Employee agrees that, during the Term and for a period of two (2) years hereafter, Employee shall not directly or indirectly own, manage, operate, control, participate in the management, administration or control of, lend employee's name to, or maintain or continue any interest whatsoever in any enterprise (a) having to do with the provision, distribution, marketing, promotion, or advertising of any type(s) of service(s) or product(s) in competition with Employer within a radius of one hundred (100) miles from Hospital or (b) offering any type(s) of service(s) or product(s) similar to those offered by Employer within said radius.

13. This contract constitutes the entire agreement between the parties and contains all the agreements between them with respect to the subject matter hereof. It also supersedes any and all other agreements or contracts, either oral or written, between the parties with respect to the subject matter hereof.

*14. Arbitration. Any controversy or claim arising out of, or relating to, this agreement or the breach thereof, shall be settled by arbitration in accordance with the provision of the State of _____ and judgment upon the award rendered may be entered in any court having jurisdiction thereof. The expenses of arbitration shall be borne by the losing party or in such proportions as the arbitrators shall decide.

15. Death During Employment. If Employee dies during the Term of this Agreement, Employer shall pay to the estate of Employee the compensation which would otherwise be payable to Employee up to the end of the month in which Employee's death occurs.

16. Except as otherwise specifically provided, the terms and conditions of this contract may be amended at any time by mutual agreement of the parties, provided that before any agreement shall be valid or effective it shall have been reduced to writing and signed by the Chairman of the Board and _____ _____.

17. The invalidity or unenforceability of any particular provisions of this contract shall not affect its other provisions, and this contract shall be construed in all respects as if such invalid or unenforceable provision had been omitted.

18. This agreement shall be binding upon the Hospital, its successors and assigns, including without limitation, any corporation into which the Hospital may be merged or by which it may be acquired, and shall inure to the benefit of _____ _____, his/her administrators, executors, legatees, heirs and assigns.

19. This agreement shall be construed and enforced under and in accordance with the laws of the State of _____.

This contract signed this _____ day of _____, 19___.

(NAME OF HOSPITAL)

BY: _____
(Chairman of the Board)

WITNESS:_____   _____
(Name of Individual)

WITNESS: _____

Addendum A:
Duties of the Chief Executive Officer

His/her duties shall specifically include supervision of personnel and financial matters, attendance at meetings of the Board and its Executive Committee, reports to both bodies concerning all phases of the operation of the Hospital, including as well services rendered in connection with the operation of the Hospital, employment of personnel and acquisition of machinery and equipment. Employee is hereby vested with authority to act on behalf of the Board in keeping with policies adopted by the Board, as amended from time to time. In addition, he/she shall perform in the same manner any specific duties assigned or delegated to him/her by the Board.

9

Starting Off on the Right Foot

The beginning is the most important part of the work.

—Plato

This chapter assumes that you have followed my advice and worked hard on your job search—sending out professional and focused resumes, networking extensively, interviewing and following up, working with search firms—and, lo and behold, landed a great job. You then accepted the offer and negotiated a favorable contract. Well, what else is there? Simple, roll up your sleeves and get to work, right? Wrong. Even the finest candidates can get into trouble when starting off in a new job.

Practical Tips

In a sense, beginning your new position is a continuation of your job search. If you don't fit into the organization, you may lose the job you worked so hard to win. To prevent that from happening, I have some practical and prudent tips, which will ease your entry into the organization and safeguard your continued success.

Take Your Time

You might have big plans, but hold off on implementing them too soon after your arrival.

Assess the Management Style and Organizational Philosophy

How do they do things? Who really runs the show? The ability to adjust to the organization's culture is vital to men and women alike, but can pose particular difficulties for women who are working primarily with male colleagues. The first few months may seem like a trip across a mine field, but you want to focus on fitting in. If you view your new colleagues as allies, and not adversaries, you minimize a potential problem. In a study conducted by the Center of Creative Leadership in San Diego, the difficulties associated with becoming part of the culture of the new workplace were the primary reason for derailment among women executives. My advice here echoes a major theme of this book: You rarely go wrong with a positive and professional attitude.

Keep Your Mouth Shut

More politely, listen to what others say. Pay attention to what the problems are. Even though the organization may be in trouble, new employees usually have a honeymoon period. Use this time wisely.

Gather Information

You can continue the data gathering you did before you were hired now that you are inside. Read in your spare time to find out all you can about your new organization and your particular function within it.

Avoid Intrigue

Resist getting involved in any political intrigue or gossip. As the new person, you may be approached by people eager to tell you the inside scoop, but you need to avoid this without seeming self-righteous.

Be Courteous and Friendly to Everyone

Organizations tend to be very hierarchical, yet in your dealings with all levels—board members, superiors, peers, medical staff, and subordinates—you should be equally respectful and professional. Your conduct toward all colleagues should be above reproach.

Conduct Yourself Professionally

Discriminatory harassment, which includes sexual harassment, is a serious problem in the workplace, yet some people are still unclear about just what constitutes an inappropriate or offensive remark. When in doubt, cut it out. Also, telling ethnic or off-color jokes may jeopardize others' opinions of you. You don't have to be a stuffed shirt, but you want to be businesslike and conduct yourself ethically. When we hear the term "sexual harassment," we usually think of someone demanding sexual favors as a condition for employment, but it is also sexual harassment when an employee creates a hostile environment by speech or behavior. If you want more information, see the end of the chapter for some further reading or read the organization's employment policy.

Be Visible

Be out and about an hour daily meeting with people. Meet and greet the night shift. Let people know who you are. Learn their names.

Focus on the Work at Hand

Start doing what you do best, solving problems and getting things done. Before you know it, you will feel at ease. You can now become an indispensable part of the organization.

Resist Importing Too Many Ideas and People from Your Past Organization

People quickly tire of hearing how great things were where you used to work. If they were so great, why aren't you still there? There is hardly any organization that doesn't have some value. By constantly referring to your past experience, you indirectly put down your current organization. Along these same lines, if you begin a hiring spree by recruiting employees from your old organization, you risk (1) alienating your former employer, (2) creating a clique of people who think and act the same way, and (3) offending the employees in the current organization whose support you need.

Examples

I have included two examples roughly based on actual people whom I have known. In the first, the candidate successfully made the transition into the new organization. In the second, the person didn't work out and was let go.

Example 1

Joe's tenure as CEO of a somewhat troubled hospital had been rocky and he was eventually forced to resign. After a thorough search, he eventually took a job as COO in a larger hospital, working for Barney. Joe was careful to make sure that Barney was informed if any issues cropped up with the medical staff. He was also careful not to upstage the CEO, who was naturally concerned whether Joe could make the transition back to COO. In all his dealings with the doctors and the administrative staff, Joe worked to make sure that he was perceived as supporting the CEO. Any disagreements he and the CEO had were worked out behind closed doors and never discussed elsewhere. In this way, Joe successfully came to be viewed as a respected and effective part of the leadership team at the new hospital.

Example 2

Mike reported as COO to Ben, the CEO, but his recruitment had been forced on Ben by the president of the multihospital system. During the course of the interviews, Mike never informed Ben that he was a heavy smoker, although the fact that the hospital was smoke-free had come up during the interview small talk. After he started working at the new hospital, Mike was frequently seen on the patio with the rank-and-file workers who smoked. This practice irritated Ben, who never confronted Mike about it. In Ben's opinion, smoking outside looked bad, and someone could think that Mike was talking with employees about inappropriate matters. In fact, Mike did no such thing. But in this situation, appearances mattered more than the truth, and Ben's impression of Mike was irreparably damaged. They failed to establish a good working relationship, and Mike was let go. Fitting in can be just as important as getting into an organization.

Ending the Job Search

At the same time that you begin your new job, you also wind down your job search. I have some common sense suggestions on how to smoothly end the process that you have so vigorously pursued. Although you have borne the burden and responsibility of your job search, you have been helped by many individuals. As a courtesy to them, you should let them know that you have succeeded in finding the right job. Notify all the members of your network once you have accepted a position. Deactivate your candidacy with other organizations, and celebrate your success.

Shutting Down Your Network

Notifying all the contacts in your network gives them the satisfaction of knowing that you found a suitable position and allows them to update your record in their network files. You should also use this opportunity to thank them for their contribution to your success. Appendix 9.1 shows a letter that can be customized for each of the individuals who assisted in your job search. Use your TNT records to ensure that you remember the names of all the individuals with whom you discussed your job search.

Deactivating Your Candidacy

Deactivating your candidacy is an important follow-up task to carry out. Quite probably you are still being considered for other positions. You owe it to those other organizations to alert them of your decision to accept another position. From their perspective, you are still in the running unless you tell them otherwise.

Celebrate!

Reward yourself. This step may sound obvious, but many health care administrators are so involved in their work that they are not used to taking time to be self-indulgent. Mark this significant accomplishment with a three-day weekend at a nice resort, a well-deserved celebration. Go out and buy a new piece of sports equipment, a new briefcase, or a pricey gadget that you really want. It doesn't matter what you do or buy, but take the time and make the effort to celebrate your success. You have undergone a rigorous and at times demoralizing process—and you emerged triumphant.

After you have successfully found your new job, show your family your appreciation for their moral support and cooperation during the job search. If you have the money and time for a family vacation, you may want to schedule one. In a study we conducted, the majority of health care professionals named time with family as a valued way to spend their free time. The same study suggests that health care professionals view vacation as a favored free-time activity. If you cannot take the time to go right now, start planning an extraspecial trip for the whole family later.

Suggested Reading on Sexual Harassment

Bravo, Ellen, and Ellen Cassedy. *The 9 to 5 Guide to Combatting Sexual Harassment* (New York: John Wiley, 1992).

McCann, Nancy, and Thomas A. McGinn. *Harassed: 100 Women Define Inappropriate Behavior in the Workplace* (Homewood, Illinois: Business One Irwin, 1992).

Petrocelli, William, and Barbara Kate Repa. *Sexual Harassment on the Job: A Self-Help Law Book* (Berkeley: Nolo Press, 1992).

Appendix 9.1

Sample Letter Notifying Contacts of Your New Position

December 17, 1994

Michael Anderson
Director
Healthcare Associates
The Franklin Building Suite 200
Philadelphia, PA 19153

Dear Michael:

I am writing to thank you again for your time and interest in my job search in September. Your suggestion that I speak with Sister Margaret Booth of Sisters of Charity Hospital was a strong lead. My efforts resulted in my accepting a position with an affiliated organization, East Hills Passavant Hospital, where I have been hired as the Budget Director. My new address as of January 15, 1995:

East Hills Passavant Hospital
4985 East Hills Parkway
Pittsburgh, PA 15305
(412) 376-0789

Again, thank you for your help.

Sincerely,

Richard Overachiever

Part IV

Creating Opportunities

10

Making the Transition from the Military

All that is human must retrograde if it does not advance
—Edward Gibbon

This chapter addresses the special case of those men and women whose professional lives have been spent in the military and now, whether for personal reasons or as a result of reduced military spending, are preparing to move into the private sector. I offer many practical points to consider on writing the resume, dressing for the interview, and casting your military experience in the most positive light for your prospective employer.

If you are retiring from your military position as you read this, you are off to a late start. Ideally, you should strategically situate yourself a year in advance. If that is not possible, you can still start immediately to capitalize on your military experience.

Benefits of a Military Career

As you begin your job search in civilian life, you may experience some negative assumptions about the military. To combat any prejudice you may encounter, emphasize some of the winning attitudes that you bring with you from the military:

- A can-do stance toward problem solving
- Adaptability, or grace under pressure
- Teamwork

You also have the advantage in two highly touted management buzzwords: quality assurance and cost containment. The military's efforts in total quality management (TQM) have led to an aggressive pursuit of quality assurance throughout operations. As a military person, you are probably head and shoulders above civilians who hold comparable positions when it comes to quality assurance. Here is a fact to consider: The American Hospital Association went to the Navy for its protocols in establishing quality assurance, so the military must be doing it right.

Although in the past military hospitals did not always have to watch costs, like payroll, with the same sharp eye as civilian hospitals, the recent cutbacks in military spending have forced military hospital administrators to contain costs zealously. Remember the many concrete ways that you have helped your health care facility save dollars. You have the experience from your years in the military and you should capitalize on it.

Recall how tight your travel budget was as a military officer. As a result, you are probably more conscientious about travel expenses than your civilian counterpart. And, when you have been offered that excellent position and you are negotiating for salary and moving expenses, remember that the military will pay for your relocation when you retire. Use this as a bargaining tool when you are at the table.

Books and Resources for the Military Person

The United Services Automobile Association publishes a guide, *Transitioning from the Military to Civilian,* which members can order by calling (800) 531-8753. This guide covers all types of work, but is nevertheless very helpful. Included is a bibliography for further reading.

The Retired Officers Association (TROA) offers a placement service for members. Make use of it along with all the excellent services TROA provides. TROA also publishes a pamphlet (with bibliography) called *Marketing Yourself for a Second Career.* If you are a member, call (703) 549-2311 to order your copy or write to The Retired Officers Association, 201 N. Washington Street, Alexandria, VA 22314-9975.

Also, many military bases sponsor retirement/career development seminars. Start attending these seminars in advance of your scheduled departure.

The Department of Defense is offering an exciting new program, Operation Transition. This program works to help service members and their spouses make the switch to civilian life. Operation Transition includes two automated employment assistance programs that registered employers can use to find qualified employees: the Defense Outplacement Referral System (DORS) and the Transition Bulletin Board (TBB).

DORS is a mini-resume registry and referral system that gives employers access to military people looking for civilian employment. The system started in December 1991 and its data base increases daily. Be sure it includes your current resume.

By using TBB, registered employers can place job ads on an electronic bulletin board. The number for employers to call is (800) 727-3677. Check with your service branch transition office for the current job listings.

Operation Transition and its automated transition systems came about from the 1991 Defense Authorization Act, P.L. 101-510. This legislation requires the Secretary of Defense to provide employment assistance to separating service members and their spouses. The Navy, Marine Corps, and Air Force offer these transition services from their family centers; the Army has set up separate transition assistance offices for this purpose. Since your country has pledged to help you and your spouse find suitable work in the private sector, take advantage of programs such as these and take pride in the contribution you have made in your country's service. Your military background is a real plus, and you may find it opens doors for you in your job search.

Maintaining Contacts in Civilian Health Care

You have already made contacts in civilian health care, every day on the job. The best contacts are people who are familiar with your work. Say you are the patient care director at your military base hospital. Every time there is an unusual set of circumstances surrounding a patient's death, you must work with the local coroner. He or she can comment on your character and professionalism. Another source of contacts with civilians in a related field is the many physicians you have worked with over the years. Some may currently be in private practice. Stay in contact with these individuals after they leave the military and you will have a built-in set of references when the time arises. An advantage of this approach is that if you have strong working relationships with physicians you will be sought after by civilian employers.

Writing the Resume

A military background might seem to lend itself to the functional resume format, but I advise you to prepare a historical resume and carefully describe your duties in a way that would make sense to a civilian reader. If you are inexperienced in writing a resume, speak to the human resources officer, follow the guidelines in my book, and show it to friends who work in high-level jobs in the private sector. Ask them to be blunt; after all, you want your resume to be as professional as possible. During your job search, cultivate an appearance of sophistication concerning your career development. Be aware that you must always maintain the competitive edge.

Incorporating Your Fitness Reports

Fortunately for you, military record keeping gives you a built-in data base for listing your skills and accomplishments—the fitness reports. Before you leave, obtain copies of your fitness reports and read them carefully, highlighting those comments that would favorably impress an employer. Unlike your civilian competitor, you can literally back up your claims that you managed to improve a specific aspect of your job performance in a six-month period because your commanding officer noted it. More importantly, these reports jog your memory and provide a supply of meaningful accomplishments to list on your resume and discuss during the interview.

Preparing for the Interview

Do your homework. Be current on career literature and consult the directory of the American College of Healthcare Executives. Find out about the individuals with whom you will be interviewing. You can go to any library and conduct a literature search on anyone who is an affiliate of the American College of Healthcare Executives. Read their publications. I have a colleague with 23 years in the military who made flash cards of the interviewing committee members. During his interview, he dazzled everyone with the ease with which he remembered names, professional backgrounds, and hometowns. Find out all you can about the organization for which you would be working. In addition to reading this book, read a general management book that has received strong reviews so that you can discuss topical issues. You want to convey the impression of a person who is sophisticated and well-read in general business and career development.

Focusing on Your Appearance

In terms of appearance, I have some very direct remarks about appearance that may or may not apply to you. Some of the dead giveaways of a military person in civilian clothes in the job market are the military haircut, military eyeglasses, the sports watch, and the blended fabric suit. Perhaps because military people are so accustomed to looking crisp and professional in their uniforms, they are overly lax when it comes to dressing for civilian life. Don't kid yourself—we are judged on our appearance. As Pubilius Syrus said in the first century B.C., "A good exterior is a silent recommendation." Hospitals and health care organizations have unwritten dress codes, which you must be aware of and follow. Think of this way of dressing as a uniform. The money and time you invest in acquiring the uniform is worth the effort.

Starting at the top, you need to go to a hair stylist off the base. Health care is conservative, so you don't want to allow your hair to be overly long if you are a man, or extravagantly styled if you are a woman. You do want to have professionally cut hair that does not reinforce the civilian's preconception of the military haircut.

If you wear eyeglasses, you may have a favorite pair with military frames. Keep those for working around the house; order a new, more stylish pair for your job search. You may consider buying contact lenses, but all you really need is a classy, flattering set of eyeglasses. This out-of-pocket expense is worth every dime—besides ophthalmologists recommend having prescriptions checked on a regular basis.

You may own a very serviceable sports watch that is accurate to the nanosecond. However, before you begin your job search, you need to spring for a new watch. Purchase a gold-tone watch with a leather band. You need not spend a fortune—an elegant understated watch can cost as little as $100. That subtle detail indicates that you know how to dress.

Finally, you need to buy a few new suits or well-tailored dresses, as the case may be. The focus here is on 100 percent natural fibers and expert tailoring. These new clothes will become your new professional uniform, so research what that uniform is. Spend a morning in the most prestigious clothiers in town, and walk through the business district. Notice what people are wearing. If you can find a shop that discounts top-quality professional clothing, buy your clothes there. If not, head back to the tony, stuffy shop and invest what may seem like a small fortune. The money spent on good clothes is actually a necessary expense. The overall impression you want to project is that of a quality individual, with conservative and impeccable taste.

A final point about shoes: Fellows, buy yourself a pair of leather wing tips. Ladies, buy a pair of high-quality leather dress shoes. Draw on your military training and shine those shoes. This job search is a different kind of boot camp, but the drill sergeant is no less exacting.

All these details matter: knowing the benefits of a military background, using the available transition and retraining services, maintaining and capitalizing on civilian contacts, writing the resume, incorporating fitness reports, preparing for the interview, and focusing on your appearance. Finding a new job is a full-scale operation and requires the attention to detail and single-mindedness that served you well in your military training. Now it's time to translate these skills to civilian work.

Survey of Former Members of the Military

Our firm recently surveyed people who left the military in the past five years and now work in civilian health care to find out about their successful job searches. They represented the branches of the armed services as follows: 43 percent Army, 38 percent Air Force, and 19 percent Navy. The average length of service was 22 years in the military, and 40 percent of the respondents currently hold CEO, COO, or VP level positions in civilian health care. When we asked them to rank the most beneficial techniques in finding out about jobs, the top two responses were networking with civilians that you already knew (63 percent) and networking with former military that you already knew (62 percent).

And what was the least beneficial technique? Well, 64 percent identified waiting for employers to call as the least beneficial to them in finding out about jobs. This survey reinforces what I have already said about the importance of networking and should motivate you to work the contacts you have made during your military career.

Another significant finding was that 72 percent secured their first job before leaving the military; the remaining 28 percent, after leaving the military. However, the average length of the job search was seven months for those who found jobs while still in the military, and two months for those who found jobs after having already left. These statistics suggest that people can work harder at finding a job once they are no longer employed, but I still recommend starting your job search before you leave, to minimize the gap in your employment history and to maintain your momentum for the job search.

Our survey confirms that military personnel can successfully compete for jobs in civilian health care—over one third of the respondents have already been promoted. These men and women positioned themselves while still in the military and effectively used their contacts, both civilian and military, to find good jobs in health care administration.

11

Lifting the Glass Ceiling: Interviews with Executive Women

It is impossible for me, a white male, to walk in the shoes of a woman or member of a minority group seeking to build a career in health care administration. Therefore, I called twelve prominent individuals, both women and minorities, and asked them for their advice. I chose people whom I knew something about and whose professional accomplishments are beyond question. Chapters 11 and 12 reveal the results of those conversations.

A great deal of career literature focuses on the difficulty women face "breaking the glass ceiling" and "staying off the mommy track." In spite of the difficulties women face as they balance the demands of family life with career responsibilities, the number of women working in health care administration is increasing.

Demographers estimate that women and minority males will comprise two-thirds of the American labor force by the turn of the millennium. Women now represent over half of the students in M.H.A. programs nationwide, as well as in other professional programs like law, medicine, and accounting. In the future, health care will no longer be dominated by men. As experienced women achieve responsible positions, they will become mentors and role models for entry-level administrators of either sex. In time, a candidate's gender will very likely be a nonissue.

A leader in the charge for change is the American College of Healthcare Executives. In 1991, the American College of Healthcare Executives published a study, co-authored by researchers at the

University of Iowa's graduate program in Hospital and Health Administration, called "Gender and Careers in Healthcare Management: Findings of a National Survey of Healthcare Executives."[1] The study statistically assesses the current situation in health care administration, concluding that opportunities for women are increasing. The American College of Healthcare Executives has also helped to sponsor groups of women health care executives and women's health networks, providing funding for these ventures. In July 1992, the College adopted a new code of ethics, which explicitly discusses nondiscriminatory guidelines in Section II (c).

As I emphasize throughout this book, professionalism and a strong work ethic rarely fail to build a career in health care. As a job candidate, a woman may feel that she is dancing through a mine field, but if she is bright, highly skilled, and hard-working, she can win over most hiring committees, and, in turn, most board members, colleagues, supervisors, and subordinates. It would be naive to say that there are no impediments to a woman pursuing a career in health care. There are ways, however, to minimize their effects.

When possible, participate in professional organizations. You will not only stay informed on the current issues, which may or may not pertain to you, but you will also learn how to conduct yourself as a professional and have opportunities for leadership roles. If you are active in a women's professional organization, you can also discuss any frustration you may feel when you encounter sexism in your work that you cannot ignore, but that would jeopardize your career path if you were to respond by taking legal action. More senior women can offer strategies in this setting as well.

In all the professions—engineering, law, medicine, politics, academia, and the military—ambitious and highly motivated women have felt the sting of being the outsider. I don't want to minimize the hostility some women face. However, I do believe a good defense is a strong offense. When all else fails, let the person know that you will not be intimidated. Initiate harassment proceedings only as a last resort, since unfortunately they can put the victim at risk of being labeled a troublemaker.

In addition, you have your work cut out for you if you are pursuing a high-level position while raising children. I raised my kids when roles were more traditionally defined, and no one marveled at my ability to be a good father *and* a successful business executive. A double standard persists toward professional women who are parents. Avoid being pigeonholed as a working mom. You are a professional who happens to have kids. Talk about them if someone asks, but strive to maintain the line between your roles as administrator and parent.

Most people, women and men alike, have a photograph or a few personal mementoes on their desk, but you don't want to overdo it in a way that detracts from your professionalism.

Interviews with Women in Health Care Administration

I interviewed six women who have achieved top positions in health care administration. Their success stories are inspiring and useful. Because traditional social roles differ for women and men, I also asked these women about their own experiences concerning marriage and family. As more than one of these top executives notes, you must make informed, conscious decisions on both personal and professional issues.

I want to thank these respondents, who appear in alphabetical order, again for their contributions and candor. I have the greatest respect for their professionalism.

Susan Croushore, Vice President of Operations, Medical College of Pennsylvania Hospitals, Main Clinical Campus

Career path and personal outlook on women in the profession. Susan has a graduate degree in science and an M.B.A. She began her career in health care as a researcher and clinician and switched to administration five years ago. She sees opportunities for women in health care increasing at a greater rate than in such fields as accounting. The individuals in her organization are committed to professional advancement for women, and she encourages you to seek out similar organizations in which to work and succeed.

Stereotypes. One negative stereotype that she encounters is that women are perceived as neither interested nor skilled in technical matters. At the American College of Healthcare Executives Conference on Information Systems, at least six or seven vendors expressed amazement that she, a woman, was even there. She replied that of course she was interested in knowing about computers and let it go at that. Another group of people likely to hold negative stereotypes toward her as a woman are some of the public officials whom she encounters. At meetings with her, they look for their male counterparts, and immediately assume that they can delegate the secretarial role to her. "Don't buy into their attitudes," says Susan. "These people waste your time."

One positive stereotype she has felt is that she is a role model. After she received her promotion, she was gratified at the number of people, especially women and lab personnel, who look up to her professionally. She thinks you need to feel comfortable with both kinds of reactions if you are serious about advancing in your career.

Biggest hurdle. Her greatest challenge has been balancing her professional and personal responsibilities, which include children. In spite of the extra work, Susan does believe that she can manage her professional and personal life, but notes that she has a very supportive spouse, as did all the respondents who are parents.

Advice to "up and comers." Find a mentor. This person, whose ethics must be similar to yours, can help in four areas: education, establishing contacts, serving as a role model, and identifying managerial style. She credits her two mentors with much of her professional success. Get support systems in place. She emphasizes quality of personal relationships over quantity. Have friends and family members you can really talk to. Establish a presence in professional organizations. Be reliable, selective, and visible. And always think like a winner.

Breaking through the glass ceiling. "Have confidence to carry out your professional goals. If at times, it seems like you have to work twice as hard, then just work that much harder. Complaining won't get you noticed, but hard work will," Susan asserts. Her solution to avoiding the glass ceiling was to work in an academic hospital that had traditionally recognized women in medicine, where she believed gender bias would be less likely.

Kathryn E. Johnson, President and CEO,
The Healthcare Forum, and Executive Publisher,
The Healthcare Forum Journal

Career path and personal outlook on women in the profession.
Kathryn heads the Healthcare Forum, an international organization
that researches and teaches leadership strategies to individuals and
organizations. She has held her high-profile job for seventeen years
and, in fact, was instrumental in reshaping the Healthcare Forum's
goals and expanding its membership at a critical juncture in 1986.
She received a B.A. from Indiana University at Bloomington, and a
master's in organizational behavior from Boston University. After
working for six months as the director of education of what was then
the Association of Western Hospitals, Kathryn was asked to become
the CEO when he resigned. She refers to this opportunity 17 years
ago as a fortuitous event. She acknowledges that such cases cannot
be planned, but recommends being mentally and professionally
prepared for them.

According to Kathryn, women in health care have three distinct
advantages over their female counterparts in corporate America.
First, women in health care have a range of professional avenues,
from nonhospital settings to managed care to insurance. Second,
women have more role models at the executive, decision-making level
of health care; she cites as examples the key female health care
figures in the last two presidential administrations. Seeing women in
leadership roles encourages other women to envision similar possibilities for themselves. And the third advantage is that health care is
especially receptive to women.

Stereotypes. Kathryn thinks that stereotypes persist, but she has too
much to do to worry about them. She does caution women starting
out to be aware that they may encounter them. She herself found
some stereotypes early on; she thinks that many of those uncomfortable situations occurred as a result of awkwardness rather than
rudeness. The stereotypes have weakened during the past twenty-five
years, she states, as so many women are knocking people's socks off
with their accomplishments.

Kathryn's professional background in organizational behavior
has given her a great deal of wisdom and savvy about handling any

stereotype. If a situation is off course, bring it out into the open and clarify what is going on, she advises. Confront the unreasonable person who attempts to limit you by making assumptions about you and your abilities based on gender.

Biggest hurdle. The decision to radically reshape the Healthcare Forum in 1986 has been Kathryn's greatest hurdle to date, but gender did not play a part. However, as the CEO of an organization in transition, she did have to manage a series of changes and conflicts—a leadership role few women had held at that point. She says the board's decision placed the Healthcare Forum on the line financially. Yet the strategy worked; the Healthcare Forum has been growing at almost 30 percent a year. Kathryn admits that this reorganization was enormously risky, but the outcome has been rewarding.

In the past, women were socialized to avoid conflict and to do the safe thing. But leadership requires undertaking potentially "make or break" steps, while maintaining the necessary enthusiasm and commitment. Her organization, founded in 1927 as the Western Hospitals Association, had been a regional acute care association. Now expanded internationally, the Healthcare Forum includes the Executive Education series and research and publications focused on health care leadership for the future. Kathryn created a professional hurdle, worked hard, and vaulted herself and her organization into a powerful position in health care.

Advice to "up and comers." Be a strong networker. Leadership can be a lonely role, so seek out the intellectual and moral support that you may need. Invest in your own intellectual development. Focus strategically on professional goals. Be clear on your values. Present yourself in a positive and proactive way, without overstatement. Above all else, Kathryn urges, focus on your performance. What works and accomplishes the job is the acid test. By making things happen, you can devise your own strategy for succeeding in whatever area of health care administration best matches your strengths and vision.

Breaking through the glass ceiling. Kathryn believes that a glass ceiling exists, but that it is being broken every single business day. Women in health care perform important jobs well, which does not surprise Kathryn. "Women and men have the same cultural background, and women have the same capacity to act in leadership roles." The glass ceiling will soon be an anachronism, particularly in health care.

Joanne Judge, President of Community Hospital of Lancaster

Career path and personal outlook on women in the profession. A recent highlight in Joanne's career was her term as chair of Healthcare Financial Management Association (HFMA) in 1992. She acquired the necessary financial skills early on; Joanne began her career in public accounting, quickly specializing in health care, before moving to finance in health care. She believes that health care is an ideal career choice for women and men alike. Women often have the team-oriented management style that health care is currently seeking; she notes trends like medical groups, managed care, and community care networks. In her current position as the president at Community Hospital of Lancaster, Pennsylvania, she feels that health care administration is a great career choice because she can directly influence people's lives. Joanne notes an altruism found in health care that is not found in manufacturing, or even other service industries. She is exceedingly optimistic about careers in health care and believes women and minorities will do well.

Stereotypes. Joanne has sidestepped negative stereotypes. She candidly notes that she capitalized on the solo role. When she did or said something, she thinks co-workers noticed. As an undergraduate in the first class of women in a formerly all men's college, Joanne had a strong sense of self. Because she began in public accounting, where she experienced greater gender bias in the firm and with clients, Joanne has actually had little trouble with negative stereotypes in health care administration. Her credibility was her expertise. One stereotype that she is eager to see fade is the solo role, as when she was described as "the first woman chair of the Chamber of Commerce." In that particular case, she corrected the journalist and reminded him that she was actually the second woman to serve in that capacity.

After she was chosen to be the president, Joanne asked the chair of the search committee if her gender had had any negative bearing on the decision. He gave her a blank look and said that, no, actually, they hadn't given it a thought, but they were a little concerned about her relative youth.

Biggest hurdle. Indirectly, her greatest hurdle did hinge on her gender: success in her career had an inverse relationship with success in her marriage—this does not only happen to successful women, but to successful men as well. She believes that women and men alike must be clear on their goals, responsibilities, and expectations in their marriages.

In her role as a mentor to college women, she tells how a young woman explained to Joanne that she was terrible with directions and that therefore her boyfriend was going to pick her up from her mentoring meeting with Joanne. Joanne stressed to this young woman and to women in general: Do not allow social pressures and expectations of helplessness to limit you personally or professionally. Never act helpless.

Advice to "up and comers." Be broad-based. Stretch yourself. When she volunteered to head the new family services clinic, thereby moving from a staff to a line function, she gained the experience to move from finance to operations. Recommend yourself. Create a good network, both within the industry and especially outside of it. She believes that serving on the board of the YMCA builds a greater network than serving on the board of the Diabetes Society. She also said something interesting about being a woman: You don't have to imitate a man to succeed. You don't have to dress like a man, pursue "masculine" interests like sports (unless you are genuinely interested), or try to be someone you are not. Be professional and be yourself.

Breaking through the glass ceiling. Yes, it exists, in her view. "Where you cannot break it, leave the organization to find one whose style matches your own." Joanne notes that an autocratic management style manifests itself in more ways than just the glass ceiling. Assess whether an organization promotes women. If it seems not to, determine whether you can pursue your goals better elsewhere.

Kathryn J. McDonagh, President, St. Joseph's Hospital of Atlanta

Career path and personal outlook on women in the profession. Kathryn's career path illustrates her personal commitment to influencing people's lives. She began as a nurse, completed her B.S., earned a master's in nursing, and embarked on a deliberate move to her current job as president of a 346-bed hospital. She has also written two books, including *Patient-Centered Hospital Care: Reform from Within*, published by Health Administration Press. Her professional success is no overnight fairy tale transformation. As Kathy herself says, "I had a master plan as early as in the ninth grade to do great things in health care." In her view, the professional advancement of women will be guaranteed when more women from traditionally "female" occupations become policymakers and leaders.

Stereotypes. As a negative stereotype, Kathy cites the assumption that woman cannot lead. At times, administrators were very blatant about not wanting to work with a woman. The positive stereotype that she has encountered is that women are perceived as essentially more nurturing and soft-hearted than men; this positive stereotype, however, is connected to a negative one, that being compassionate and empathic automatically precludes one from being an effective decision maker and leader. She balances her compassion with quick judgment and, as far as I can tell, has consistently earned the respect of people with whom she works.

Her response to stereotypes is direct confrontation. She has a very open, direct approach to people. In the short term, this approach can cause strife, but it leads to long-term gain.

Biggest hurdle. Kathy faced not so much a single big hurdle but rather a series of small challenges of being an ambitious woman in a profession, and a society as a whole, in which most leadership positions are held by men. "I have killed myself to be here," says Kathy. She shows no signs, nor do any of our respondents, of letting up on her drive to excel. She enjoys seeing the influence that she has had.

Advice to "up-and-comers." Educate yourself. To attain a leadership position, she believes that you need at least a master's degree. Skills development is crucial. Maximize the strengths you have been given. Reach beyond your skills. Seek mentorship. Kathy also advocates web leadership rather than the pyramid style of leadership. In her 1990 book, *Nursing Shared Governance,* which she self-published, she amplifies her argument that there are new ways of leadership. Be the hands-down best candidate.

Breaking through the glass ceiling. She believes that the glass ceiling exists, but she also believes that by acting like a leader, you can become one. "Always be calm in a crisis, always upbeat, always smiling, always the leader." In the boardroom, she uses humor to explain the big picture, which gets a good response.

She has actually had people say, "You are taking a job away from a white man. Women are not emotionally consistent enough to lead." Her force of character, belief in her goals, and optimistic approach to problem solving, however, have all enabled her to hammer away at the glass ceiling.

Pamela Kuhl Meyer, President and CEO, Edward Hospital

Career path and personal outlook on women in the profession. Growing up in a two-physician household, Pamela decided that she wanted to run the hospital—to get things done so the medical staff could do their jobs. Pamela's focused career path included an M.H.A. and a steady climb within one organization up to COO (in which she successfully negotiated a part-time workweek when her children were very young), before going after the CEO job she wanted at the hospital where she currently serves as president and CEO.

She traded financial compensation during her term as director of special projects and assistant administrator for greater flexibility and exceeded the job definitions at both positions. She therefore received promotions at an accelerated rate. She acknowledges that it demanded a lot from her and required an organization that valued her work enough to cooperate, but she believes if a person makes herself indispensable, then one's bargaining power on such issues increases. She accepted any "crummy jobs"—setting up a copy center, completing CONs, and trouble shooting—in a succession of line jobs for six years. When she had finished, she had overseen most types of crises and had established credibility. She knew she wanted to run a hospital even before she started college, because her physician parents had steeped her in health care, but she wanted less of an around-the-clock commitment than they had. Ironically, she notes that in the twenty years she has worked in the field, the work load of hospital execs has increased.

The outlook for young women is best for those who land an operations job ASAP, even if the first job is a traditionally "woman's" specialty, such as human resources or planning. Pursue jobs that allow you to run things. The time she negotiated an end to a food slowdown that threatened to shut down operations was an opportunity to prove that she could tackle any problem.

Stereotypes. During meetings, early in her career, Pamela was assigned the task of taking minutes; she would comply, with the suggestion that the group members rotate the responsibility. By taking this approach, she showed her willingness to do what needed to be done, while diplomatically stating that the others should also share the task. In time, her colleagues were less likely to ask her to assume that responsibility.

She handled a similar stereotyping in project assignments. Again, starting out, she was rarely assigned construction projects, but rather projects in traditionally female-oriented areas such as ob/ gyn or pediatrics. A consummate deal maker, Pamela would agree to the assignment—she never turns down an assignment—but would also ask for another in a more male-dominated area as well.

Biggest hurdle. There were two hurdles early on: The first, dealing with the occasional difficult individual, does not pertain to gender. Pamela learned to stand up to the person attempting to intimidate her, as well as to tolerate disagreement, without personalizing the conflict. The second one, raising three children while pursuing a high-powered career, does have to do with gender, or rather socialized gender roles, but she overcame this hurdle by marrying a "well-chosen spouse," who assumed equal parenting responsibilities.

Advice to "up-and-comers." Assume full accountability for achieving your career goals, Pamela emphasizes. For women, keep the chip off your shoulder when you get turned down for a job. It is nearly impossible to know if you didn't get the job because you were female, or if you lacked skills or attributes that were required. Identify an area of improvement, and go after the next challenge. Be prepared. Use humor to work through controversy. Exhibit the utmost intelligence, fortitude, and hard work, while assuming risks, even when you have less than perfect information. In general, she sees the successful administrator's job as becoming increasingly complicated, and the quick, cool thinker can deliver.

Breaking through the glass ceiling. Pamela sees the glass ceiling as a self-perpetuating problem that is slowly being solved as more women wield power at the very highest levels of organizations, including boards; at these higher levels, networking among women will increase gradually. She serves on the Illinois Governor's Task Force on Healthcare Reform and is a paid member of the Gary-Wheaton Bank Board of Directors; in these contexts, she believes that speaking openly and forcefully at meetings, exhibiting confidence, and acknowledging the occasional bad call have worked for her as far as getting through the glass ceiling, and she encourages you to believe that you, as an individual, can break through it, too. She also seeks ways to make it easier for other women to get through the glass ceiling in her organization and in her service work.

Diane Peterson, Governor-at-Large, American College of Healthcare Executives, and President, D. Peterson and Associates

Career path and personal outlook on women in the profession. Even though the majority of her 20-year career has been spent in senior management positions in large hospital systems, Diane believes that future health care opportunities for women will be found outside of hospitals. Diane earned a master's in Public Health, specializing in hospital administration. She then moved to hospital operations/line management for eight years, spent six years in staff positions dealing with business development, and then founded her own consulting company seven years ago.

She recommends that women consider the broad range of management specialties, including positions in managed care, outpatient settings, the quality/service improvement field, rural health care, and physician practice management. The women—and men—who look for windows of opportunities like these and identify what they enjoy, as well as what the field requires, will succeed, predicts this owner of a management consulting firm based in Houston.

Stereotypes. Diane has a remarkably upbeat response to negative stereotypes. She rarely gets offended and takes chauvinistic remarks in stride. For example, after presenting a proposal for strategic planning to a small-town hospital authority board, she was told by the board's legal counsel, "You did a right good job up there [at the lectern]. You're real purty . . . and smart, too!" Women who have been in the field a number of years will undoubtedly be able to recall similar instances in which direct reference was made to their appearance with a bluntness that may shock those of you just entering professional life. Often the stereotype is that attractive women cannot be bright or competent, much less accomplished leaders. Adding to this is the cultural practice of focusing on women's appearance more critically than men's.

One negative stereotype she has encountered is that highly placed women in health care do not help other women. She disagrees, noting that she expends a lot of effort in helping women advance. Whenever possible, she directs business to other women. When executive recruiters call, she makes it a practice to have the names of three strong women candidates to volunteer. She believes that this stereotype results from the fact that networking among women professionals is only now evolving.

As far as positive stereotypes go, Diane recalls turning her gender into a career builder when her CEO needed someone to work with physicians. "Peterson can handle it," became an often-heard phrase. In Diane's opinion, physicians tend to work better with female administrators. Asked to explain this seemingly chauvinistic remark, she noted, "Physicians are accustomed to working with nurses and other professional women who *listen* to them!"

Biggest hurdle. When Diane attempted to capitalize her own company, one bank turned her down for the completely collateralized line of credit she wanted to establish. She simply wanted to borrow against her own $50,000 certificate of deposit to establish a banking relationship. Although this setback was temporary—she called another bank and got her line of credit from a loan officer who happened to be a woman—she still recalls this incident with some rancor, since it appears that her gender worked against her. It is interesting to note that Diane, who is a "self-professed optimist," cannot recall any similar gender-related hurdles in her health care professional life.

Advice to "up-and-comers." Be outstanding. Be willing to be noticed. Take some risks. Stand out in the crowd. Pick mentors carefully, and change mentors when you need to. (In her 20-year career, Diane has changed mentors four times, and still has one.) Build and cultivate a list of contacts. "People are pathways in the profession," says Diane, whose computerized mailing list contains over 1,800 names. She takes every opportunity to keep in touch with these people, to build friendships and careers. She sends birthday cards to many of them and routinely writes notes commending journal authors, seminar speakers, and recipients of industry awards.

Be political. Be strategic. Volunteer for tasks that bring name recognition and responsibility, such as editing the quarterly newsletter of the professional society. Do *not* volunteer to arrange the in-house holiday party.

Breaking through the glass ceiling. Diane believes that the glass ceiling does exist. She broke through it by starting her own company in 1987. She believes that in a soft employment market, search committees and potential employers will be less willing to hire or promote women and minorities to executive positions. If the job market improves or health care executive salaries decline, the glass ceiling may cease to exclude women from top positions.

Diane cautions against pursuing too narrow a specialty. When search committees look for individuals for the top spots, they seek those with strong track records and exceptional interpersonal skills. Strong technical expertise, say, in finance, must be balanced with demonstrated leadership skills. She acknowledges that this equation does not have a simple solution, but it demands constant effort to excel on the part of the candidate.

Note

1. "Gender and Careers in Healthcare Management: Findings of a National Survey of Healthcare Executives," American College of Healthcare Executives and the Graduate Program in Hospital and Health Administration, University of Iowa, 1991.

12

Beyond Racial Barriers: Interviews with African American Health Care Executives

Because patients in the health care system represent every racial, ethnic, and religious group in the United States, one might expect that health care administration would also reflect this diversity. However, like management in most other industries, administration in health care is not representative of society. Recent efforts by organizations like the American College of Healthcare Executives to promote diversity and encourage members of minority groups to pursue careers in health administration show an important new commitment to change. This chapter addresses the current climate, conditions, and attitudes faced by members of minorities in health administration. It focuses in particular on the experiences and expectations of African Americans and includes interviews with six successful African American health care executives.

In 1990, the American College of Healthcare Executives issued a public policy statement asserting its intention to increase opportunities for minorities in the profession of health care administration (see Appendix 12.1). If you are a member of a minority group and you are pursuing a career in health administration, you should look at this document as a firm promise by the professional society of health care management that you have a future in the profession.

Despite this new commitment, however, it may be some time before we can say that equal opportunities truly exist. We need a concerted effort to put theory into practice. As is the case for women, the paucity of highly placed administrators from any minority group still impedes the progress of those just starting out. Why is this the case? First, because with the exception of members of religious orders, who have a distinct career path, women and members of minorities with aspirations for top jobs historically have had few role models (although before desegregation, there were black administrators in so-called black hospitals). It is role models, mentors, and contacts putting in a good word for a candidate who can make the difference. Role models are very important in career development, especially in the early stages. Mentors help when needed, and good contacts can open doors (see Chapter 4).

Second, and quite unfortunately, research shows that among whites there is more support for preferential hiring for women than for ethnic and racial minorities. Because of these attitudes, you may receive different treatment, even though such treatment is illegal and unethical. Although ideally affirmative action policies would counteract such tendencies, in practice that is not always the case.

One important study, "Shaping the Organizational Context for Black American Inclusion," reviews the problems that arise at the recruitment, entry, and promotional stages for African Americans. The researchers identify three possible biases:

1. Negative racial stereotypes
2. The solo role, when you are the only African American in the work group
3. The token role, when, as a new employee, you are viewed by co-workers as incompetent merely because you have been hired under an affirmative action policy

In turn, the following barriers arise:

- Biased and stressed recruitment practices
- Assumed dissimilarity and exaggerated expectations on entry
- Polarized evaluations of performance[1]

Researchers at Johns Hopkins University concur with these findings. They investigated institutional barriers faced by African Americans at three stages of employment—the job candidate (which is my main focus), the job entry stage, and the job promotion stage. In a study of 4,078 employers covering a nationally representative sampling of jobs, four types of exclusionary barriers were investigated.

- Segregated networks at the candidate stage
- Information bias at the entry stage
- Statistical discrimination at the entry stage
- Internal markets at the promotion stage[2]

As an African American health care administrator, it is easy to read these research results, or perhaps just reflect on your own experience, and get discouraged or bitter. But I would suggest that you should keep these barriers in mind as you pursue your career goals in health care and find ways to overcome them. One of the best ways to overcome stereotypes is by allowing people to know you and your work. Particularly at the candidate stage, you need to network aggressively.

My number one strategy for finding a great job in health care is networking. But make sure that you do not limit yourself to networking with members of the ever-growing African American professional class. Because health care is one field in which blacks are particularly underrepresented in the management ranks, you are doing yourself a disservice by not networking across racial lines. Dr. Peter Weil, FACHE, and Nat Wesley, FACHE, who both worked on the study, recommend belonging to both the American College of Healthcare Executives and NAHSE as a way to maximize your professional network.

The most significant study on opportunities for African Americans in health care administration, "A Racial Comparison of Career Attainment in Healthcare Management: Findings of a National Survey of Black and White Executives," was conducted jointly by the American College of Healthcare Executives and the National Association of Health Service Executives and published in 1993. Its three objectives were to compare career attainments, account for any differences, and consider social policies that might redress any inequities discovered. The study quantifies differences and sheds light on this issue with a solid statistical foundation. Everyone in health care administration can learn from the anonymous responses of 853 health care executives, black and white, on the often gray issue of race.

To follow up, we spoke with a few of the lead researchers, Peter Weil, Ph.D., of the American College of Healthcare Executives, and Nat Wesley, Kevin Lofton, and Howard Jessamy of NAHSE. The comments of Nat, Kevin, and Howard, who are also members of the

American College of Healthcare Executives, can be found in their respective interviews.

Peter describes the difference in focus between the ACHE/ NAHSE study and the following six profiles as follows: In grade school, most of us were part of a group picture, with some in the first row, some in the middle, and some in the top. The study is like a group picture of 853 administrators. In contrast, the six profiles of outstanding African Americans who have achieved a high degree of professional achievement, found in the following section, are like individual snapshots. These six people demonstrate the range of successful strategies for minorities who aspire to executive positions in health care.

Peter is optimistic about increased opportunities for minorities in health care administration. The American College of Healthcare Executives is no longer an "old boys' club", so he encourages minority women and men to join. He also has some general insights for everyone leaving a graduate program and just starting out: "Any ambitious individual must substitute the risk-taking spirit needed in real-life hospital management for the spirit of inquiry cultivated in a graduate program. Grab the earliest possible chance to test yourself as a manager. Ideally, one should marry a single discipline with an assistant departmental job rather than executive assistant to gain executive experience." This advice pertains especially to African Americans, who typically serve in staff positions such as finance, which do not offer enough opportunities for running a department or a program, and who therefore miss the management experience needed for advancement to top-level positions.

Interviews with African Americans in Health Care Administration

I interviewed six African Americans who have achieved top positions in health care administration. I hope you can benefit from their success stories. Because I am interested in how theory can be transformed into practice, I asked these people about their own experiences with achieving professional success in the competitive world of health care employment. Significantly, all six acknowledge that African Americans face varying degrees of discrimination, but they have found strategies for overcoming attitudinal barriers.

Howard Jessamy, President of the National Association of Health Services Executives, and President, District of Columbia Hospital Association

Career path and general outlook on minorities in the profession. Currently, Howard is the president of the District of Columbia Hospital Association, and the first African American to head one of the 52 state and district hospital associations in the United States and Puerto Rico. Since earning an M.H.A. from the University of Michigan in 1972, he has held a series of leadership positions in health care organizations, from his successful turnaround of the troubled Mound Bayou Community Hospital in the mid-1970s to his 1993 election as president of the National Association of Health Services Executives (NAHSE). He has steadily built his career and professional reputation.

Outlook for minorities in the profession. Howard encourages you to view the entire spectrum of health care administration as you seek opportunities. The underrepresentation of racial minorities exists in all areas, and likewise the opportunities for professional advancement. Despite the decreasing number of traditional hospitals, Howard remains bullish on institutional organizations. The growth areas of managed care and health care financing—whether traditional insurance or the system that will follow health care reform—will provide new positions for minorities as well.

Stereotypes. Minority candidates face positive and negative racial stereotypes, which may surface more once they are on the job. The positive stereotype is the "Jackie Robinson figure," which Howard explains is the expectation of being an immediate superstar. He handles that by always trying to do his best. One negative stereotype he sees is that because he is an African American male, people assume he is an avid sports fan. In one meeting, a professional colleague jokingly suggested *Sports Illustrated* was a journal of black enterprise that they should use to raise majority awareness of the minority professional class. Howard and everyone present responded with silence, which let the person know that his joke was ill-advised and the stereotype unwelcome. You can let people know that you don't like racial stereotypes in a variety of ways, by either saying nothing, as Howard did here, or by telling them directly. Or, you may use a humorous reply to convey your reaction. As Howard says, how people handle negative stereotypes is highly subjective. Find a way that works for you in a given situation.

"Interact, not isolate," recommends Howard when handling the stereotype that minorities don't network across racial lines. The American College of Healthcare Executives/NAHSE study points out that the lack of informal socializing can impede the professional networking of minorities. Howard makes an important distinction between social self-segregation and sanctioned segregation. If you don't want to be part of the group at a nonworking lunch, you don't have to force yourself to join in. But you should participate in organizationwide activities, such as group outings or holiday parties. "A good manager will make the rounds," says Howard. You can combat all stereotypes by allowing others to know you, as an individual, with your own preferences, shortcomings, and strengths.

Another stereotype he sees is the channeling of minorities to support service rather than clinical settings. Also, you may encounter the stereotype that minorities have succeeded or can only succeed in the public sector. Respond to these stereotypes rationally. For example, in the public versus private sector debate, you can argue that, in the past, the publicly funded health care organizations were more apt to act affirmatively. Whatever the stereotype, do not allow others to limit you.

Biggest hurdle. Howard has experienced two big hurdles. The first one may or may not be race-neutral: he moved around a great deal and was often asked, "Why are you leaving your organization already?" He moved to advance his career. The second obstacle, responding to the "right fit" argument, does pertain to race. Whenever he applies for a new position, makes it through the process, and does not get the position, Howard asks for a critique to learn areas of improvement. Years ago, he was told that there wasn't the "right fit," which he interpreted as that particular organization's unwillingness to hire a minority at the senior level. He has heard this same response several times since. Nonetheless, Howard did not lose his focus, nor his ambition, nor his optimism. He kept working. In his view, there is an attitudinal barrier against racial minorities at the CEO level, which he compares to the glass ceiling faced by women executives. This barrier has become easier to cross in the last three years, so he urges you to keep interviewing and to keep striving, so that as organizations do become more willing to recruit and promote racial minorities, you will be one of those individuals in demand.

Advice to "up-and-comers." Select internal and external mentors. (These individuals need not be members of a minority group to benefit you.) Consider professional opportunities outside of the traditional organizations. Build a reputation as both a generalist *and* a specialist. Right now, specialists have an edge, but the leadership requirements include the generalist's perspective. Achieve this balance by asking for responsibilities outside your area of expertise and by acquiring management skills in your continuing education and professional development. If necessary, strengthen your communication skills. There is a bias against minorities at the professional level because some majority colleagues may not have worked with minority professionals before. To be competitive, any candidate must speak and write well, especially minority candidates. Do not underestimate the value of community service. When you do apply at majority organizations, use your involvement as a selling point. Your commitment to the community that your organization serves reflects well on it, as well as on yourself.

Handling the "solo" and "token" roles. The likelihood that you will be the first, or the only, minority to have held a particular position is decreasing all the time. Still, you just have to handle the pressure, says Howard. Being a trailblazer carries an additional burden. If race makes you metaphorically and literally visible, Howard believes that you must "stretch up" to the expectations of others in your organization, for your sake as well as other minorities who follow you.

"We didn't get here by ourselves; we are standing on other people's shoulders," says Howard, in tribute to both the leaders of the civil rights movement and the founders of NAHSE such as Haynes Rice. As you attain leadership roles, you can build relationships with the politics of inclusion. When he was the first African American administrator at a majority hospital, Howard recalls that a couple of the managers sat back waiting to see if they would sabotage or support him. In time, by his efforts, they supported him. He succeeded.

Identifying oneself as a minority in employment correspondence. You should certainly identify yourself in the professional correspondence as a member of a racial minority for two reasons, advises Howard. First, it is better for the search consultant or hiring committee to know that you are an African American sooner rather than later. Second, in some instances, this may be a selling point for getting an interview. To best convey this fact professionally, Howard recommends the understated approach. For example, list your membership in NAHSE, or a black sorority, or the leadership position in a civic group that serves the minority community. In this way, you focus on your accomplishments *and* represent who you are at the same time.

Robert Johnson, Executive Vice President and COO, Detroit Medical Center

Career path and general outlook on minorities in the profession. Because he credits his six years as an Air Force officer with starting him off, Bob's career path overlaps with some of the information from Chapter 10, "Making the Transition from the Military." He believes the military is an excellent place for minorities to build leadership skills. His current position, the EVP/COO of a private, not-for-profit seven-hospital health care system, marks a shift from a succession of highly visible jobs in increasingly larger public sector hospitals and health systems. He eventually became CEO of four large public hospitals before taking his current job, in which he works for an old graduate school buddy.

Bob believes that, despite the sluggish job market, the outlook for minorities in healthcare is better now than ever before. The National Association of Health Service Executives celebrated its twenty-fifth anniversary in 1993, the numbers of minority women and men in healthcare administration are increasing, and those health executives who will market themselves to all types of hospitals in the United States will land jobs. In his view, one limits the universe of opportunity by looking solely at the approximately 100 urban public hospitals in the United States. Bob thinks that public and private organizations have different benefits and different challenges, but you must be open to working in either setting.

Stereotypes. "If *you* think you can't do something, then you won't," says Bob, who believes that you can move beyond the negative and positive stereotypes of African Americans that unarguably exist and that worsen in tough economic times. He deals with stereotypes by not allowing them to constrain or limit his dreams and goals.

Biggest hurdle. In his career, he has not encountered a major setback, although he did feel somewhat isolated socially while serving in the military. Bob chooses to see opportunity in that adversity, because it gave him experience in tough situations.

Advice to "up-and-comers." Know yourself. Associate with people whose values and ideas you respect and who in turn respect you. Don't personalize bigotry, he argues, for prejudice is part of the human condition, be it racial, religious, ethnic, or gender based. Prejudice is not to be tolerated, yet it is not all encompassing. As Bob puts it, "We all have prejudices and preconceived notions; we need to work at not allowing them to become barriers to recognizing people's abilities, strengths, and weaknesses. However, when confronted with prejudice, don't allow the anger or disappointment to be the central driver."

He does believe that, as a professional who is a racial minority, he has obligations to the community, which he fulfills by challenging fellow leaders to address minority underrepresentation and prejudice. Bob encourages you to serve on a variety of committees—civic, social, and, of course, professional. "Go to the meetings and speak up."

Handling the "solo" and "token" roles. On occasion, Bob notes, you must take on the role of one of the few minority administrators in a predominantly nonminority hospital. Attitudes vary in different geographical regions, organizations, and communities. Because there is a limited number of professional openings, you might have to bear the temporary discomfort of being the only African American in the group, but if the reality is that you want the job in question, then by all means, take it. He is also very mission-driven about working to bring about increased numbers of minorities in the profession, so that the terms "solo" and "token" become meaningless.

Identifying oneself as a minority in employment correspondence. Be upfront and proud about your racial identity, urges Bob. He notes that realistically your resume might indicate that you are a member of a minority, say, by your holding a position in a traditionally

African American service or civic organization, such as NAHSE or the NAACP, or a degree from a historically African American university. Consider the issue of race as a neutral. "Do not attempt to hide your race, nor try to use it as a calling card."

Kevin Lofton, CEO of the University of Alabama at Birmingham Hospital

Career path and general outlook on minorities in the profession. Because Kevin recently crossed over from a traditionally minority hospital to a university hospital in a southern city that was the scene of one of the major civil rights struggles of the 1960s, he has a unique vantage point on minorities in the profession. His impressive career includes being chosen 1993 Young Healthcare Executive of the Year by the American College of Healthcare Executives and turning around one hospital from a $16.2 million deficit to an $1.3 million surplus.

Stereotypes. As far as positive stereotypes, Kevin distinguishes between his professional role and his community role. In the workplace, he highlights the management team effort and plays down his individual success. As a role model in the community, he stresses his own accomplishments in terms of his race and working-class background.

Negative stereotypes surface, but Kevin responds quickly and directly. Case in point: As an administrator in a Florida hospital, he had his authority challenged by a hospital security officer. The director of security's boss, a senior hospital administrator, tried to intimidate Kevin, saying, "We just beat a black guy up in the parking lot." Without skipping a beat, Kevin replied, "He must have been a lot smaller than you are, because you are not kicking any butt this way." From that day on, every officer in the building knew who he was. Usually, Kevin maintains a professional demeanor, but in that situation, he shot right back at the offending person, talking at his level when he had to. Choose such moments, but do not allow others to use stereotypes or bigotry against you.

Biggest hurdle. His greatest obstacle, lack of money to attend graduate school, was not related to race. Kevin held a variety of jobs, including driving a cab in New York, to cover costs. He applied for every scholarship he could find, but decided he had to turn down the

M.H.A. program at Georgia State University; later on the very day he had made that decision, he received two scholarships, which allowed him to attend graduate school after all. I would like to note that this turnaround was the result of planning, not luck; to get a scholarship, you have to apply and you have to be competitive.

Advice to "up-and-comers." Stabilize your professional position before you marry. Kevin lived in five states in a five-year period during his twenties, so it made sense to wait; now he is married to a physician and they have two kids. Aggressively pursue civic responsibilities. Be mobile if it helps your career. Be visible in the African-American community; Kevin finds this very personally rewarding. Never turn down assignments on the job. Make yourself indispensable. Master physician relations. Land a first job in a line position— you have your sights set on an executive position; he passed up two staff jobs early on. Run things (in his case, ambulatory care) in order to gain experience and credibility.

Handling the "solo" and "token" roles. At Kevin's job level, race does not hinder him. Once you reach a point, people respect you and your work. Recently, he received a great deal of positive publicity— even celebrity—in the nation's capital, where he was the executive director of Howard University Hospital, and in his new home in Birmingham. Kevin would like to see the concepts of "token" and "solo" end, and he works hard in organizations to be fair and go to bat when, as in one case, he saw a person getting squeezed out solely on the basis of her race. Kevin sees the ripple effect of highly successful people, where by example and influence, people in his position can open doors and put to rest old barriers. If anything, he thinks his youth was tougher for subordinates and civic leaders to accept as he was advancing professionally than being one of a small number of high-level African American health care executives.

Identifying oneself as a minority in employment correspondence. Weigh the relevance of an item on your resume. If people want to screen you because you are African American, you probably don't want to work in their organization. Kevin is diplomatically blunt when headhunters call and asks if they are just going through the motions.

Kevin did have a bad experience when he applied for a residency back in 1978. All systems were go, until the CEO figured out that he was African American because he had listed an African American student organization under his college experience. The graduate program director at Georgia State told Kevin what had happened. Kevin responded by going after and landing another residency and never looked back. He established professional momentum and credibility and correctly assumed that being African American would cease to be a liability.

Nathanial Wesley, FACHE, Director of Planning, Howard University Hospital

Career path and general outlook on minorities in the profession: Nat offers a great deal of insight to young people in healthcare management. He is one of the senior advisers to the National Association of Health Services Executives and a fellow of the American College of Healthcare Executives. He has supported and continued many of the initiatives begun by Haynes Rice, who started the NAHSE work-study program in the 1970s. Nat has worked 22 years in a variety of health care delivery systems and academic programs. His managerial skills, administrative talents, and innate intellectualism have been strengths as he has weaved a career of management, educating, and consulting.

Nat's optimism surfaces as he expresses hope for increased opportunities for young African American health care managers. He sees opportunities on the horizon for those people who are well trained, have outstanding interpersonal skills, are willing to relocate, and who can adapt to the ongoing changes in health care administration by seeking opportunities outside of traditional hospital settings. Private health care companies such as Baxter, ServiceMaster, and Johnson & Johnson have expressed a strong commitment to increase opportunities for minorities. Time will tell if these companies are sincere about this commitment. In both private and public sectors, there will be increased professional employment opportunities for African Americans. Not enough, he cautions, but progress that will serve the entire health industry well.

Stereotypes. Nat reminds us that African American health care executives suffer from the positive stereotype of what Nat calls the "Jackie Robinson syndrome." Some whites expect that minority persons who pioneer in any field must be significantly more skilled, more talented, and more tolerant than others who are given a similar opportunity. Almost all African American health care executive pioneers, including Everett V. Fox, Elliott Roberts, Haynes Rice, and Henry Whyte, experienced this syndrome.

Nat feels that the timing of one's response to negative racial stereotyping is critical. It is important to select the right time to become retaliatory or reconciliatory. He chooses the optimal opportunity to respond to a negative stereotype. Whether it's one-on-one in an office, in a group setting, or an organizational meeting, he believes that there will almost always be that perfect moment to expose the ignorance and stupidity of racial and cultural stereotyping.

Biggest hurdle. The biggest hurdle in Nat's career was dealing with personal decisions that affected his career. He regrets not having remained within one organization for an extended period of time, because he believes you can have the greatest influence within an organization through reasonable longevity. Because Nat has held several management positions in different organizations, he has been a catalyst at the expense of having a longer-lasting organizational effect. He considers the highlights of his career to be his leadership in opening the ambulatory care center at Southwest Detroit Hospital in 1974 and his tenure on the faculties of Meharry Medical College and Howard University.

Advice to "up-and-comers." Nat feels that young health care professionals should seek a compatibility match between their persona and professional discipline. Don't become a square peg trying desperately to fit into a round hole. Your personality and lifestyle should be compatible with the requirements and demands of your professional responsibilities and vice versa. However, he advises that hanging tough in a job that you may not love for at least 18–24 months will result in credibility in seeking your next position. Young health care professionals should consider staff positions in early career development. Focus on the future development of your career rather than complaining about where you are at the moment. As Haynes Rice told Nat when he was a Young Turk starting out, "You have to pay your dues."

Handling the "solo" and "token" roles. Never forget where you are and who you are. As Nat says, "Never forget that there is a multiplicity of reasons for you having the job that you have." He encourages minority managers and executives to bring other minority individuals along and work to get your organization to move beyond looking at African American health care professionals as either exceptions or tokens. The African American or minority professional has to be committed to excellence in performance at all times. African American executives in isolated situations should always seek counsel and advice from others when confronted with a controversial or difficult dilemma where culturally diverse attitudes are at stake.

Nat likes NAHSE's goal of establishing and maintaining a pipeline of potential health care professionals by recruitment and retention activities from the very earliest stages of career development.

Identifying oneself as a minority in employment correspondence. "Answer when asked." This is Nat's response to the issue of what to disclose when applying for a position. Inclusion of extremely personal or sociodemographic data on the resume is ill-advised, says Nat. Most of the time, the professional recruiters and human resource directors will know from your professional affiliations and career tracking what ethnic or racial group you belong to. The greatest emphasis in resume writing should be your education, experience, and expertise. The health industry will be well served when all persons with requisite qualifications will be given appropriate opportunities to compete for employment.

Denise Williams, President and CEO, Roseland Community Hospital

Career path and general outlook on minorities in the profession. Denise, who was the American College of Healthcare Executives Young Administrator of the Year in 1990, became CEO at the age of 34. She had graduated from the Medical College of Virginia and had been a fellow at the University of Michigan Hospitals and Medical School. She readily admits that she had to move around a great deal in order to get so far so fast. She loves what she does, but believes that for racial minorities, relocation is even more necessary than for whites. In her view, "we are eligible for 'Black jobs' only," by which she means high-level opportunities are available to African Americans when and only when the institution or organization is ready to hire a racial minority.

Stereotypes. Denise does not have time for stereotypes. She cannot imagine being anyone else than who she is. Being an African American woman is very much a part of her identity. She has a remarkably confident, competent, and commanding presence that wins people over. She uses humor whenever she is asked which makes it harder to break the glass ceiling, being a woman or a minority, noting that it could be her left-handedness, thereby high-lighting how limiting stereotypes really are. During the interview for this book, she asked, "Now, am I a being featured as a Black or as a woman?" Obviously, she is both, but more importantly, Denise is a CEO.

Biggest hurdle. She has not had one biggest hurdle. Throughout her professional career, she has been very methodical and focused. At the onset, she set a personal goal of becoming a CEO by age 36 and she made that goal. One fact about her background that she believes prepared her for the competition is that, as the youngest in a close-knit family of eight boys and four girls, she became quite used to competing for what she wanted, and she does so in a straightforward, nonthreatening way. "I like working with the guys," she laughs. Her interactions with her male colleagues and subordinates, from medical malpractice attorneys to maintenance workers, are very positive. Her focus and ambition have enabled her to personally overcome the minor challenges that anyone, regardless of gender or race, must face professionally.

Advice to "up-and-comers." Plan ahead. Deliberate. Capitalize on any and all breaks that come your way. Hire people who are smarter than you! As a CEO, you will be delegating a great deal, and you need to have top-notch individuals working for you. For women and men alike, she recommends weighing all the competing demands carefully before deciding to marry and have children. Her husband, a physician, has a strong interest in her success and shares the responsibility in raising their three children.

Handling the "solo" and "token" roles. Denise tells a couple of stories about the solo role. At a bank board meeting, another board member pointedly asked her to volunteer for a special committee geared toward a minority issue. She turned it down, politely conveying that she did not want to be part of a show. At another meeting, she was complimented for having done a particular project that in fact had been done by an African American woman who worked for the bank, but who was not on the board. Denise acknowledges that this confusion could be a simple mistake, but at the same time, it illustrates some people's attitude that African Americans are interchangeable.

Denise pays tribute to the accomplishments of Florence Gaynor Everett, one of the first woman executives in health care. The decades bring change slowly, and now it's the professional successes of Sandra Austin, Marie Cameron, Deborah Lee-Eddie, and Alva Wheatley that are putting the old solo and token roles to rest. Being a CEO requires much independence and strong ego, so being viewed in these roles shouldn't faze you.

Identifying oneself as a minority in employment correspondence. Denise recommends omitting any demographic information from one's resume, but at the same time, including any leadership roles one might have held in African American organizations such as NAHSE or a similar professional group.

She did have a bad experience in the mid 1980s at a southern philanthropic hospital, when she was recruited for the CEO job based solely on her resume. Denise is convinced that the interviewing committee had no idea that she was African American until they actually met her. She also sensed immediately that she was not going to be considered seriously for the position. Denise chalks that interview up to experience and points out that it was in her best interests to cut her losses, accept the rejection, and go on to the next interview. Emphasizing that the decision to identify oneself as a racial minority is subjective, she contends that the most important part of your employment correspondence is your professional record. She believes that you are who you are, and that you should neither play down nor play up race.

Ruth Williams-Brinkley, Associate Administrator,
Operations and Chief Nursing Officer,
University of Alabama, Birmingham

Career path and general outlook on minorities in the profession. Ruth epitomizes the winning attitude that my book is about. She currently serves as the vice president of nursing in an 863-bed hospital system, where she has accountability for revenues of over $250 million. She continues to set goals for herself, including becoming a CEO. Ruth has what traditionally were considered to be three strikes against her: She is African American, she is female, and she began as a nurse. What you first notice about Ruth, however, is her professionalism. Like the other eleven people whom we talked to, Ruth firmly believes in herself and her abilities. She thinks that you must declare yourself early in your career. Nurses, for example, should specialize in either ambulatory or acute care; pick a specialty, master it quickly, and then master the business or financial side of patient care delivery. She has never seen herself as disadvantaged, which explains why no one else has ever told her that she cannot do something. In her view, any person with the work ethic and strength of will can aspire to and attain leadership positions in health care administration.

Stereotypes. With any stereotype, Ruth responds with educating herself and the other person, and working to get results that will silence any negative stereotypes. For example, early on she was the evening supervisor, when a helicopter needed to land without a landing pad anywhere nearby. She took charge and handled the situation. Ruth has had to overcome the stereotype that nurses don't know finance. She has overcome the stereotype that African Americans don't work hard by managing to work full-time, raise two children, receive a master's degree, and participate in civic and professional organizations. And by her proven leadership, she demonstrates that leadership ability does not correlate to a certain part of the human gene. Like many highly successful executives, Ruth is the first-born in her family, which may have helped to develop her independence. But that is another book.

Biggest hurdle. In January 1993, Ruth participated in an extremely unpopular dismantling of the "Baylor Plan" at her hospital. Her name and salary were published in the city paper, and she took a lot of heat. She faced this adversity by reflecting on the soundness of the decision and by refusing to personalize the negative reaction. This hurdle was not related to race.

Advice to "up-and-comers." Ruth herself was named an "Up and Comer" by *Modern Healthcare* in 1989. First and foremost, she recommends that you excel in the job you were hired to do. Focus on the actual work responsibilities, but at the same time, maintain a high profile outside your organization. Educate yourself, but limit yourself to no more than two or three conferences per year because you cannot perform your job responsibilities well if you are frequently absent from the workplace. Answer every phone call. Interview annually, just to keep sharp. Do not allow people to become complacent or accept mediocrity in the organization. Know who you are and what you want, but remain flexible and open to new opportunities.

In your personal life, be flexible. Ruth and her husband, for example, have a successful commuter marriage. In your professional life, be comfortable drawing attention to your successes in a matter-of-fact way, but give appropriate credit to others as well, because no successes are achieved single-handedly.

Handling the "solo" and "token" roles. By her example, Ruth advises you to keep so busy that you don't have time to notice if people are reacting to your race or gender. She also espouses the Golden Rule—by treating others with respect, she guarantees that she will be treated the same way. Be independent in your thinking and maintain personal and professional integrity. If you are yourself, people will recognize and respond to excellence in your job performance, and the rewards will follow. As she puts it, "I never considered myself as disadvantaged or unfairly treated." She does recall feeling proud when she switched to management and other African Americans employees expressed delight in her accomplishments. She believes that their delight was directly related to the fact that she always remembered who she was and always treated others with kindness and respect. In this sense, being one of the few is a positive experience because you can inspire and motivate others to push themselves ahead professionally.

Identifying oneself as a minority in employment correspondence: Over the course of her professional career, Ruth has changed her mind on this issue. Initially, she would sometimes identify herself to a recruiter or potential employer as a member of a racial minority. Now, however, with 20 years of a solid record of employment and documented achievements, she believes that her accomplishments speak for her. If race becomes a factor, then the employer is likely seeking something other than achieving the stated goals for the position. Ruth does not believe that race has been a factor in determining whether she has been hired and discourages individuals from making it an issue.

Notes

1. Thomas Pettigrew and Joanne Martin, "Shaping the Organizational Context for Black American Inclusion," *Journal of Social Issues* 43 (1987): 41–78.
2. J. H. Braddock and James McPartland, "How Minorities Continue to Be Excluded from Equal Employment Opportunities: Research on Labor Markets and Institutional Barrier," *Journal of Social Issues* 43 (1987): 5–39.

Appendix 12.1

American College of Healthcare Executives Public Policy Statement July 1990

Enhancing Minority Opportunities in Healthcare Management

Statement of the Problem

Minority employment in healthcare is well established, but examination reveals it is qualitatively different from nonminority workers' employment experience. While ethnic and racial minorities represented nearly 20 percent of all hospital employees in 1985, they held only one percent of top hospital management positions such as chief executive officer, chief marketing executive or chief information officer. For example, a recent public policy poll of College affiliates suggests that African American executives among the membership number only about 2 percent.

Underrepresentation is a problem in and of itself; however, analysis of progress toward redressing this imbalance reveals the problem is becoming more acute. Following efforts in the 1970s to attract minority students to graduate study in health administration, enrollment and graduation of minorities has declined by approximately one-third since the peak year of 1979. Tracking the career experiences of those minority executives who have graduated requires relying on anecdotal sources of information as neither the College nor the Association of University Programs in Health Administration reports on race specific career data. Such sources report that career opportunities for minorities too often are limited to management positions in public institutions or private institutions serving a disproportionate share of the indigent population.

Policy Position

The American College of Healthcare Executives believes that all healthcare executives, educators, and policymakers should acknowl-

Approved by the Board of Governors of the American College of Healthcare Executives on July 27, 1990. Reprinted with permission.

edge our collective inability to maintain the gains that had been made in recruiting racial and ethnic minorities to the field of healthcare management. These groups should reaffirm their commitment to redressing the imbalance in minority representation in leadership. It is also incumbent upon us to realize that in the absence of the higher levels of federal support and leadership we once enjoyed, our challenge is greater.

The College encourages healthcare executives, educators, and policymakers to actively pursue the following:

- Institute outreach mechanisms to attract promising minority candidates to healthcare management careers.
- Endorse at every opportunity the goal of achieving full representation of minorities in healthcare management.
- Institute policies in their organizations that assure no discrimination on the basis of race or ethnicity.
- Work with minority organizations within their community to create sources for scholarships and fellowships.
- Advocate for governmental and private philanthropic programs that allow for increased funding to underwrite advanced education, information dissemination, and employment opportunities for racial and ethnic minorities.

The American College of Healthcare Executives advocates a variety of approaches to effect the representation of more ethnic and racial minorities in healthcare management.

13

Overcoming Discrimination: Personal Strategies

Everybody wins.

—Anonymous

The twelve women and men interviewed for Chapters 11 and 12 prove by example that opportunities exist for those people with the skill, drive, and commitment to take them. One encouraging note: When Lewis E. Weeks edited the *Hospital Administration Oral History Collection*, published in 1988, there were relatively few women and minorities in the field. On the other hand, I had to arbitrarily limit the profiles in this book; there were too many strong candidates to include. My principle of selection was to talk to people from a range of backgrounds to emphasize that any job candidate, of any race, ethnic group, gender, or professional expertise can devise a winning strategy. We could have interviewed many other equally gifted individuals across the country.

Let me now shift the focus to you, and how *you* can advance your own career in health care. Who knows, you may be interviewed for the twenty-first century edition of this book!

Stand out in your work—be outstanding. In addition to the twelve people profiled in this book, consider the accomplishments of, for example, General Colin Powell and Supreme Court Justice Ruth Ginsberg in the face of racial, religious, and gender bias in the military and legal professions as they ascended to top positions in their respective fields. Both these individuals are remembered by colleagues as exemplary, always the best candidate for the job. One of Ginsberg's fellow law students reminisces that she stood out even then—she was impeccably groomed when her classmates were wearing the wrinkled student garb of the late 1950s, she had an infant, and she edited the Law Review! And Powell's fellow officers have long recognized his merits.

During your job search and on the job, remember to let your light shine. The word "candidate" comes from the Latin word for "shining bright." A successful candidate shines in every way.

If you are having an especially hard time during an interview or as you start a job, remember that a sense of humor, combined with a strong sense of self, can effectively fend off unkind remarks. You may use a blank look, which can tell the person that he or she is out of bounds. Or tell the offending person firmly that you take offense at that remark. If the person persists, talk to someone in the human resources department and document the incident.

I have no idea when the day will arrive that hiring decisions will be made with no consideration, explicit or not, about a candidate's gender, race, or ethnic background. In the meantime, be aware that some, not all, employers will judge you by a different standard. Meet them with the utmost in professionalism, cooperative spirit, and pride. And deflect any unspoken racism or sexism with a thick skin and a slippery back. You want to work, and you haven't got the time or energy to be baited by the individual who resents the fact that you are a professional who happens to be a woman or a member of a minority group.

Social attitudes can act as barriers for women and minorities, restricting the opportunities that theoretically exist. However, these barriers are crumbling. There are women and members of minority groups who are proving themselves in the health care profession, and their numbers are increasing, one by one. You can advance in health care.

There are opportunities. The best candidates use the same fact-finding methods espoused throughout this book. Determine what kind of organization you are attempting to join. Maintain a positive attitude. Focus on your work. Avoid fulfilling any negative stereotyping that can be used against you. Exude confidence, and don't make self-deprecatory remarks. Women, in particular, have been socialized to minimize their accomplishments, or to credit luck, when in fact, their success results from their own efforts. Accept responsibility for your failures and demand recognition for your successes.

The Good News about Fairness in Hiring

As a society, we are becoming increasingly sophisticated about what constitutes harassment or discrimination in employment practices, including the job search. Tolerating discriminatory practices exposes companies to expensive litigation and creates a bad working environment. Companies like Employment Learning Innovations, Inc., conduct workshops to educate managers in avoiding sexual harassment and discrimination. Many organizations have EEOC specialists in-house to foster compliance and awareness. Although none of these measures guarantees that you will receive fair treatment in your job search or on the job, they suggest that the holdouts to full participation by women and minorities in the workplace may themselves be in the minority. My hunch is that the playing field is getting more even, and interviewers, colleagues, and supervisors will commit fewer fouls in the coming years. Meanwhile, be the exemplary person you are capable of being and the likelihood that race or gender will impede you will decrease. When people know and respect you, they will be forced to let go of their attitudes.

Overt vs. Unspoken Barriers

Haynes Rice, back in 1964, sat in a boardroom during the first month on the job as administrator, when one of the board members said, "I told you it was a mistake to hire a nigger." Rice, who later went on to help found NAHSE and its work-study program, which advanced the opportunities of countless young people, had the best revenge. "I went there in April, and by November, he resigned, a millionaire, but still racist."[1] That blatant degree of hostility brought out the fighter in Haynes and pushed him to work harder on winning votes in the boardroom.

An acquaintance, a female anesthesiologist, recalls an incident that occurred several years ago during her residency at a teaching hospital. She recounts it today with the wisdom that comes from success. The senior staff physician told her outright that he did not want her in the operating room, that he did not like the idea of it, and that he had opposed her being hired. Needless to say, she was thunderstruck at the time. What could she say? More importantly, what could she do? She decided not to take the bait. Her husband wanted her to take legal action, but she believed that her own best interests were better served by proving that senior physician wrong. She completed that residency and has pursued a successful medical career. Before she left, the senior staff physician called her aside and apologized for his remarks. As she put it, she lost a battle, but won a war. In her opinion, she would have risked her career by challenging him in a sex discrimination suit.

These two instances of discrimination are examples of overt resistance to the high-level participation of minorities and women in the past, both as physicians and administrators. Haynes might have been furious at being insulted, but he maintained his dignity and professionalism and actually increased his own power base. He sized up things and figured out a way to make sure he was the one who remained in the hospital. In the second incident, the physician actually preferred the senior physician's hostile honesty, compared to the hidden prejudices she sometimes experienced in the workplace. In her words, she knew where she stood. She managed to stand tall, despite his harsh words, and by her efforts win his respect.

Be a Winner, Not a Whiner

I cannot say it is easy, but maintaining a winning attitude is the best way of getting ahead. Whoever you are or whatever kind of discrimination you face, keep in mind that you are a professional first and foremost. Regardless of the demographic data you list on a census form, you are an individual job candidate as you apply for jobs in health care. Your personal fortitude will carry the day and overcome cultural biases. This book focuses on getting a great job in health care and the fact that you are reading it indicates that you have a winning attitude that marks a professional. Do not allow other people's assumptions, however cruel and unfair, to get in the way of your own goals. In the words of Epictetus, "First say to yourself what you would be; and then do what you have to do."

Note

1. Haynes Rice, "First Person: An Oral History," in Lewis E. Weeks, Ed., *Hospital Administration Oral History Collection, Lewis E. Weeks Series,* 1983, 32.

14

Maintaining Sources of Support

No man is an island, entire of itself.
—John Donne

Because, as well as being a job candidate, you are a human being with some personal responsibilities, you need to consider all of the preceding information and advice in the context of your family and support network. Few of us, even the single men and women pursuing careers in health care administration, have complete say about where we live and work. And as marriages have moved from the traditional to the egalitarian model, unilateral decisions about where a couple lives are increasingly uncommon. As I stated in the chapter on job offers, you really need to involve your partner as early as possible in your job search. If you have children, you can talk to them about your plans as the job search progresses, but your wife or husband deserves to know about your goals and plans in advance. Finally, you need to be sure that you have a system of support so that you are able to draw on the advice and expertise of others in your situation.

Traditional Families

Social scientists and psychologists have extensively researched how frequent job-related moves affect the families of corporate executives and military personnel. Their findings are helpful; they prove that the effects depend on how the move is handled. You may well have first-hand experience of what results from a relocation. Family members have to leave friends, change jobs and schools, and leave familiar and beloved communities. Although difficult to quantify, the consequences are at least disruptive if not painful.

What can the researchers suggest to help you minimize these disruptive effects of relocation? They suggest that you can anticipate the problems and work to solve them as a family. For instance, Patricia Voydanoff concludes that although frequent moves have negative effects, they can be avoided or minimized by family cohesion before the move, spousal attitude, and coping strategies.[1] The more your family participates in the decision, the smoother things go. It may take some persuasion on your part, but you have to convince them that the move will benefit everyone in the long run.

If you read the management literature on decision making, this approach may remind you of the participatory management style. Well, it should. Just as employees in corporations cooperate more fully as their sense of investment and involvement increases, so it is in families, where family members cooperate when their contribution matters. Obviously, this model needs to be adjusted: Spouses generally share family decision making as full partners, teenagers hold less power but need to be included in the discussion, grade-school children can express fears but typically adjust readily, and pre-schoolers vote with the majority, if they are even aware of any proposed relocation. Your decision to move can be made at the "executive level," but it ideally should address the concerns of all members of the family.

Recent research on hospital executives reveals that they differ slightly from business executives in general. Typically, spending time with their families is extremely important. If you value time with your family, consider everyone's happiness as you begin your job search. Although you may earn more money after the move, your family may need to get used to the new place, so you should listen to their concerns. The need for frequent moves can actually bring your family closer together as you rely more on one another, or it can drive you apart.

Two-Career Families

A dual-career marriage ups the ante in your job search. In 1986, both spouses were employed outside the home in one-half of all American marriages, and the number increases daily. Job changes requiring relocation have even greater consequences for dual-career families than for families where only one partner works outside of the home. When you accept a job in another city and your spouse has to quit a job, he or she may lose ground in terms of opportunity, seniority, salary, or pension. Meanwhile, the likelihood that you will both find excellent jobs in the same six-month period is pretty slim. It may be necessary for you to have a commuter marriage for a short period of time while you begin your new job and your spouse conducts a separate job search while still working. However you look at it, the move will require flexibility and compromise.

Regardless of whether your spouse has an established career, he or she can help or hinder your job search. On the one hand, a strong and fulfilling marriage can be your Rock of Gibraltar in the face of uncertainty about your future. On the other hand, announcing plans to relocate and change jobs without consulting your spouse can cause resentment, and the last thing you need while looking for a job is a negative spouse. An angry spouse can be rude to prospective employers, and your spouse's negativity can be communicated to your children, so then you are really outnumbered. No one likes surprises, so tell your family about your intentions before the moving van arrives at the front door. Here in the South, we have an old saying, "If Mama's not happy, nobody's happy." It's folksy, yet true.

Have I made my point? Well, a little diplomacy and preparation goes a long way. If you are committed to moving for your career, you need to let your spouse know that long before it becomes an issue. Once you decide to pursue another job, be sensitive to the other person's feelings and needs. If you are close to accepting an offer, make a site visit with your spouse. Instead of focusing on your prospective job, spend the time researching the factors that contribute to your spouse's well-being: for example, schools, types of neighborhoods, and proximity to other metropolitan areas. Possible references include the business directory, university guide, and the local chamber of commerce. It makes sense to find out as much as you can about the new community. Your enthusiasm will spread to the other person, and in turn, your children.

As the skilled labor shortage that experts predict for the 1990s appears, your job-seeking spouse may get some help from your new employer. According to Lucia Gilbert, a psychologist who has researched two-career families for the past 15 years, 75 large American corporations provide a new benefit—relocation aid for the spouse.[2] She qualifies this promising trend by noting that the assistance tends to be informal and limited—for example, paying employment agency fees—but it is something you can ask about during the serious negotiation stage. Even more promising for the two-career couple is the new trend in higher education, which may or may not spill over into health care administration. In certain cases, highly sought-after faculty members can make their recruitment contingent upon the hiring institution finding work for the spouse. Although the competitiveness of the health care employment field makes that kind of scenario unlikely, employers are responding to the concerns of the dual-career marriage and the ever-expanding effect of women in the workplace.

But what practical assistance can you offer your spouse to expedite finding a comparable position in the new location? Even in the somewhat conservative world of health care administration, you can network on your spouse's behalf. The board members are active in the professional and cultural life of your new community, and they are a logical source of contacts. By talking about your spouse's professional interests in this way, you demonstrate your commitment to his or her work.

Now let's say that you and your family have discussed the possibility of changing jobs, and all have agreed that it is time to make the move. In fact, because you have lobbied for this move, your spouse and children may actually be excited about the move and eager to make it happen. If your spouse can take your calls at home, you know you have a reliable person backing you up. Involve your children, too. Stress to them how important good phone manners and clear messages are. You are all working toward a common goal.

Single-Parent Families

If you are a single parent—whether you are the noncustodial parent, the technical way of saying you and your children live apart most of the time, or you are working and raising your children on your own—involving your children may be even more essential. If you are the noncustodial parent, your proposed relocation to another city may radically change the visitation schedule that you and your kids now enjoy. Perhaps the divorce already has caused your children to get used to seeing you only on the weekends. If your move to the East Coast requires a "holidays and summer vacation" visitation schedule, your children deserve to know about it as early as possible, and they will probably require some reassurance that you will maintain close contact with them after you move.

If you are a single parent raising children and pounding the pavement, you may need their help in some of the practical aspects of running the house to free your time up so that you can aggressively pursue your job search. Also, because a job search can wreak havoc on your emotional well-being, your children may seem like the only friendly faces you see on a discouraging day. Regardless of their ages, your children can provide real support in practical and emotional terms. (Keep in mind their relative maturity when you are really discouraged.) Talk to them about your plans and goals, involve them in the process, and you guarantee their cooperation.

Confidentiality

Regardless of your marital status, you must emphasize to your children the need for confidentiality. If you launch your job search while you are still employed, you want to limit the conversation to your home. A casual remark made by your child to a co-worker's child at the company picnic about moving to Phoenix could cause problems at your present job. Similarly, an impulsive remark from your teenage son while taking a telephone message from a potential employer may damage your possibilities. The best tactic for keeping your children involved in your job search is to be as open with your children as their level of maturity permits, while simultaneously encouraging them to be as closed about your job search with *all* outsiders as possible. When taking telephone messages, for example, stress to your children that they want "just the facts, Ma'am."

Whatever kind of marriage or family you have, whatever the children's ages, your best defense against opposition to relocation is a strong offense:

- Team spirit
- Everybody wins
- Compromise
- Love

To ignore the very fundamental issue of how a job change affects your marriage and family is only to insure that problems will occur after the relocation. With foresight, you can have your ideal professional life and a rewarding personal life as well. No one ever said it would be easy, but some couples and families do become closer following a career move that requires relocation. With some hard work and loving words during the course of your job search, you can at least hold the line. Your family life is a detail you cannot afford to overlook.

Job Search Support Networks

During the last ten years, many job search support networks have been formed across the nation. In churches and community centers, individuals from a variety of professional backgrounds meet weekly to exchange information. Membership costs are nominal, if any. These groups yield a big return on investment, if you use them wisely. You are not there to socialize, but to talk about your job search and listen to others talk about their job searches. What works? How do you change your mindset after you have been turned down for a promising position? How do you promote yourself and your job search without being overbearing? What does it mean to go after people, not jobs? These are the kinds of questions discussed at these meetings.

You probably have heard of job search support groups, or perhaps even attended one of their meetings. Job search networks provide two very useful functions—keeping you on track during your job search and bringing you in contact with others who are in your situation.

By attending a weekly meeting that focuses on job search efforts and skills, you structure your time and maintain the momentum necessary to find the right position for you. Others who work in different fields may have creative suggestions and strategies that have worked for them. You probably have a wealth of practical suggestions to share with others as well. An important part of human nature is altruism, and by helping and encouraging others, you benefit yourself.

The meetings generally last two to three hours and address one topic per session. Topics covered in a job support network may include any of the following: networking, resume writing, maintaining focus, time management, self-evaluation, interview skills, and so on. In many ways, these networks serve the same purpose as this book—telling you how to identify and successfully compete for the job you want. Unlike reading a book, however, attending a meeting about the job search puts you face to face with other people, which helps keep you on track. In addition, the groups often sponsor excellent motivational speakers. If you are like me, you may really recharge your batteries by listening to a gifted motivator. One word of caution: As with outplacement, you don't want to get too comfortable. These networks in no way replace the network you have been actively building since you first started your job search.

How do you find a job search support group? Most major city newspapers provide a weekly calendar of career-related events in the Sunday classified section, so you should start there. Churches of many denominations consider helping people with career development as a part of their ministry to the community, and therefore are active sponsors of job search support networks. The sponsoring agencies, whether they are churches or community groups like the YWCA, are nonprofit, so you should not be asked to pay.

In fact, when looking for a job search support network, be skeptical of any service that promises results and asks for anything but a nominal membership fee or contribution. (You may, for instance, be asked to chip in for coffee or to cover photocopying costs.) At this point, you already have a goal and have done the kind of self-assessment that precedes the job search, so you should not spend time and money at the career development programs offered by local colleges and universities, unless you have a particular need to address, like interviewing skills. Your best bet are the church-sponsored job search support networks. You can go on a weekly basis, or just when you feel the need to get some fresh ideas.

Spending one evening a week talking about ways to find an excellent job and the problems of being unemployed in the meantime can help to alleviate strain at home. For example, if your spouse feels the burden of listening to you, I recommend that you find a quality job search network to broaden your support system. Even someone who knows you very well may be unable to really empathize with you consistently during your job search.

Notes

1. Patricia Voydanoff, *Work and Family Life* (Newbury Park, CA: Sage Publications, 1987), 52.
2. Lucia Gilbert, *Sharing It All: The Rewards and Struggles of Two-Career Families* (New York, Plenum Press, 1988), 165.

Further Recommended Reading on Family Issues

Bastress, Frances. *The Relocating Spouse's Guide to Employment: Options and Strategies in the U.S. and Abroad* (Chevy Chase, Maryland: Woodley Publications, 1989).

Ferber, Marianne A., Brigid O'Farrell, and LaRue Allen. *Work and Family: Policies for a Changing Work Force* (Washington, D.C.: National Academy Press, 1991).

Gilbert, Lucia A. *Sharing It All: The Rewards and Struggles of Two-Career Families* (New York: Plenum Press, 1988).

Rice, David G. *Dual-Career Marriage* (New York: Macmillan Publishing, 1979).

Scanzoni, John, and Maximiliane Szinovacz. *Family Decision-Making: A Developmental Sex Role Model* (Beverly Hills, California: Sage Publications, 1980).

Vannoy-Hiller, Dana, and William W. Philliber. *Equal Partners: Successful Women in Marriage* (Newbury Park, California: Sage Publications, 1989).

Winfield, Fairlee E. *Commuter Marriage: Living Together, Apart* (New York: Columbia University Press, 1985).

15

Getting Motivated

Books are for nothing but to inspire.
—Henry David Thoreau

You now have the tools needed to conduct your job search successfully. What you bring to the process determines how quickly you will
meet your goal. At all times, you must assume that you can accom-
plish what you have decided upon. In this chapter, I will offer some
real-life examples of how sheer doggedness won out, as well as some
of my own suggestions for keeping on your charted course when
everything, from a crowded field to lagging self-confidence, threatens
to put you out of the race. After that, it is time for you to stop reading
and start doing. Good luck!

Be Resourceful

Be creative and aggressive in your pursuit of contacts. As George
Patton said, "Take calculated risks. That is quite different from being
rash." A few years ago, I was waiting for the elevator at a national
conference of the American College of Healthcare Executives when
a confident gentleman approached me and asked for five minutes of
my time. That same person is now a valued part of our team at Tyler
& Company. He had heard me talk at the same conference a year
earlier. In the interim, he had positioned himself to make the transition from the military and had actually targeted my company as the
place he wanted to work. He did his homework, and he limited
himself to five minutes, during which time he generated sufficient

interest to warrant further discussion. I realized later that part of what set this individual apart was his confidence and his foresight in being ready for an opportunity.

That story brings to mind another remarkable individual whose foresight I described in Chapter 7. As I related, the candidate had managed to get an interview at a major hospital in the state capital. En route to his interview, he visited the state planning agency where the particular hospital's certificate-of-need application was available as a matter of public record. Needless to say, after reading that and educating himself about the organization's fiscal plans, he proceeded to his interview with a wealth of information and presented himself as a person of foresight and resourcefulness.

Be resourceful—that sounds like a good idea, but how do you become resourceful? Another word for "resourceful is "adaptable." The career experts who study trends in the workplace agree that in the job market of the future, adaptability will be the hallmark of the successful job candidate. If you feel stuck in your current position and your job search is inching along slowly in spite of all your focused efforts, make the further effort of acquiring a new job-related skill. An obvious area is computer literacy. Or, if you are a mathematical wizard with a strong accounting background and only limited expertise in management, you can enroll in an organizational psychology course at the local college. Without investing in an advanced degree, you can increase your sophistication and knowledge in that area. Another idea is to volunteer for special projects at your current job—for example, a quality assurance group—if such projects will develop new skills. Choose carefully, since your time is at a premium, but invest in some type of educational endeavor. Knowledge is cumulative, and never goes to waste. As an added benefit, you keep your intellect sharp. The celebrated actor, Sir Laurence Olivier, was once asked how he managed to maintain his successful stage and film career as he got older. His reply, that he learned a new skill or craft every year, points to the importance of learning throughout our lives.

Motivation

Being motivated is especially important in making a job change. Changing jobs requires a lot of hard work, sustained over an unknown time period. It is even harder to change jobs if you are still employed; a lot of other things get in the way of making those networking calls, the essential part of your job search. If you find yourself bogged down in your search because of conflicts with your regular job, then set yourself the realistic goal of making four networking calls per day. This reasonable number keeps you focused on the task at hand. Obviously, if you are unemployed, you should be making a lot more contacts than four per day. Your target number should be between ten and fifteen daily calls where contact is made. There is a difference in the kind of motivation that corresponds to your employment status. If you have a job, you are probably motivated by ambition. If you are unemployed, necessity motivates you to keep calling. In either case, fire up your motivation and keep it burning.

Get Off Your Duff

One of my pet peeves is the individual who loses his job, receives a big severance deal, and then doesn't really look for a job until the severance pay runs out. This scenario has happened so many times in health care employment, that many of us in the recruiting and out-placement fields have begun to look upon excessive severance (longer than one year) as a potential hindrance to a candidate's getting a job. Some candidates with a cushy severance income seem to think they can take their time about looking for a job. They goof off around the house, play golf, take extended vacations, and tend the vegetable garden when they should be out making things happen. I have often heard these types say that they are taking their time, waiting for the "right thing" to come along.

I cannot emphasize how foolish this attitude of waiting for the "right thing" is. Ironically, the longer a person is out of work, the more difficult it is for that person to get any job, much less the "right thing." After a year's unemployment, they have to consider accepting the very jobs that they turned down earlier in their search for the "right thing"—if the potential employers will even talk to them. Employers tend to ask themselves if there is something wrong with the candidate who has been unemployed for an extended period of time. After a year, candidates can start to appear desperate and talk about all the times they came in number two in a search. All of these things add up to a negative impression of the out-of-work candidate. The job market for health care executives is very volatile. Many qualified and experienced people are out of work, and few new positions are being created because health care organizations are flattening their management ranks and consolidating their ventures. My advice: Get off your duff and start to work immediately to find your next job.

Perhaps one of the most frustrating things about the search process is the number of times that one gets bad news or has hopes dashed. After a number of setbacks, it is hard for a jobseeker to pick himself or herself up, dial a new telephone number, talk to another stranger, and maintain an upbeat, positive attitude. This chapter was written for those periods in your job search when you are discouraged and need a pick-me-up. Whenever you feel that you can't win for losing in your job search, return to these pages for inspiration.

Persistence and Perseverance

In conducting a job search, like any other major endeavor, one cannot overestimate the need for perseverance and persistence. To get the right number of contacts to form an effective network and find a new position requires hard work. Dogged determination is what separates the successful job search from the unsuccessful ones. I personally learned perseverance early on in my life when I started college at Georgia Tech in Atlanta. With my small-town upbringing, I had no idea of the amount of hard work necessary to succeed at this school. I was totally unprepared, intellectually and emotionally, both for the academic work and for the college professors who did not care as much about me personally as the high school teachers in my hometown. My first year nearly broke my spirit as I struggled from class to class, trying to grasp the material and keep my grade point average high enough to stay in school. As the quarters rolled on, I improved somewhat, but it was not until my junior year that I earned my first A in a class. As I look back now, the experience at Georgia Tech was my first exposure to the fundamental role played by persistence and perseverance in reaching our goals.

The lessons of persistence and perseverance have stayed with me all my life. I went on to earn my master's degree in accounting at Georgia State University and was named to Beta Alpha Psi, the accounting honors society. What makes these accomplishments especially noteworthy is that I earned my master's degree while also working 40 hours a week over the two years I was in school. Not bad for someone who barely squeaked through his first year of college. If I can do it, anyone can. All it takes is persistence and perseverance.

Not long after founding Tyler & Company, I came across the saying in Appendix 15.1. This quotation was originally attributed to Ray Kroc, who built the McDonald's Corporation, and was known as McDonald's Creed. I called McDonald's when I first saw the saying in order to get permission to reprint it. The public relations people at McDonald's told me that, although the quotation had been attributed to Kroc, he had picked it up from somewhere else. In fact, recently I have seen it attributed to Calvin Coolidge. Because I admire Ray Kroc more than Calvin Coolidge, I am still content to call it McDonald's Creed. You have our permission to reproduce it and put it on your desk to remind you always to persevere. I hope it gives you as much inspiration and drive as it has given me.

A Tale from Real Life

I include this story about my friend Mike because it demonstrates how perseverance and networking lead to success. I first met Mike when I made a call on him to do a marketing search for an HMO for which he was working as COO outside of Detroit. While we didn't get the search, Mike and I remained in contact on an occasional basis. In 1986, the group that owned the HMO decided to restructure the company and Mike, as COO, was out of a job. Mike began his networking and soon landed a job with the group health services division of a major health care company in the Southwest. Things went well for him until the parent company disbanded that division in 1987. He had been there exactly one year. Mike then resumed his networking and diligently made his phone calls. He made notes for following up and sent resumes to everyone. His networking was low key, but effective. Within a few months, Mike accepted a position in the Midwest as the director of National PPO Contracting for the planned startup of a national managed care network for a major insurance company. Mike had been on the job for one week when the insurance company reorganized internally, and Mike was left high and dry. Needless to say, he was feeling a little like Job in the Old Testament, when he asked why he had been singled out for misfortune.

Here Mike had just sent letters to all his network members, thanking everyone for helping and announcing his new job, only to find himself out of that very position! Dutifully, Mike picked up the phone and called his contacts to get his network back in motion. Within three months, Mike had a new job, his third in two years. He found a job as the CEO of a for-profit HMO in the Midwest, where he worked for four years.

Now Mike is much like you and me in many ways. But, in one area, Mike excels—he networks like a champion. In addition, Mike is the kind of person who refuses to let losing two jobs in one year through no fault of his own get him down. Surely, you can be as hard a worker at networking as Mike is.

And what does Mike have to say about his adventures in getting another job? "Finding a job is not the most pleasant situation, particularly when it results from a company restructuring. The best advice I would give anyone in this situation is to have confidence in yourself and seek out the support of your family and friends. If you focus on getting your next job and treat it as being your current job, you will succeed."

Religion as a Source of Inspiration

Many of us look to religion to comfort us in difficult times. No matter what religion we believe in, religious teachings can help us to keep our perspective. When things aren't going well, your faith may make all the difference.

In my own struggles with failure and misfortune, I often turn to the Bible for inspiration and hope. For Christians, worry is a special type of problem because worry connotes a lack of faith in God's teachings. There are plenty of indications in the Bible that worry is not appropriate for believers.

A Lighthearted Look at Worry

Why worry? There are only two reasons to worry. Either you are sick or you are well. If you are well, there is no reason to worry, but if you are sick, you again have only two things to worry about. You are either going to get better or you are going to die. If you are going to get better, there is nothing to worry about. If, on the other hand, you are going to die, then you have two things to worry about. You are either going to heaven or to hell. If you go to heaven, you have nothing to worry about. But, if you go to hell, you will be so busy saying hello to all your friends that you won't have time to worry. So, why worry?

Some Practical Advice, or, The Only Way Out Is Through

Perhaps you are reading this chapter because you have had a series of opportunities that did not pan out or you have recently been rejected for a position that you really wanted. Now you have to pick yourself up and really get back to the grindstone of networking. I have found that candidates often get a mental boost by calling a few familiar and friendly contacts. Try recreating the scene of earlier success by calling some of the people you have worked closely with. You can often receive that vital reassurance that helps repair the ego damage and moves you ahead into making those tough networking calls to strangers. Look over your list to see if there are any people you have already talked to who need a follow-up call.

And, try to get a good laugh. See a funny movie. Buy a book of cartoons. (My favorite is Calvin and Hobbes.) Listen to a funny radio station. Visit a comedy club, whatever, but find something to make you laugh. Quite seriously, laughing dispels self-defeating thoughts, puts things in perspective, and can get your job search back on track.

Inspirational Quotes

Finally, here are some encouraging observations made by people wiser than I am to increase your resolve and rekindle your confidence:

> Our best friends and our worst enemies are our thoughts. A thought can do us more good than a doctor or a banker or a faithful friend. It can also do us more harm than a brick.
>
> —Dr. Frank Crane

Too many people are thinking of security instead of opportunity. They seem more afraid of life than death.

—James F. Byrnes

Whatever task you undertake, do it with all your heart and soul. Always be courteous, never be discouraged. Beware of him that promises something for nothing. Do not blame anybody for your mistakes and failures. Do not look for approval except the consciousness of doing your best.

—Bernard M. Baruch

Sympathy is never wasted except when you give it to yourself.

—John W. Raper

What the future holds for us, depends on what *we* hold for the future. Hard-working "todays" make high-winning "tomorrows."

—William E. Holler

Appendix 15.1

McDonald's Creed

Press On

Nothing in the world can take the place of persistence. Talent will not; nothing is more common than unsuccessful men with talent. Genius will not; unrewarded genius is almost a proverb. Education alone will not; the world is full of educated derelicts. Persistence and determination alone are omnipotent.

Index

About the Author

Larry Tyler is originally from Washington, Georgia, a small town in the eastern part of the state. In 1970, he received a B.S. degree in industrial management from the Georgia Institute of Technology, and in 1973, he received a master's degree in professional accountancy from Georgia State University. He began his professional career with Price Waterhouse & Co. on the audit staff. He became a certified public accountant in 1975. In 1978, he founded Tyler & Company, which conducts searches for executives with hospitals, managed care entities, and insurance companies, for physicians in all specialties, and for physician executives. In 1988 and 1990, Tyler & Company was named by *Executive Recruiter News* as one of the top 50 search firms nationally; and in 1992 and 1993, one of the 40 largest search firms. Mr. Tyler is a fellow of the American Association of Healthcare Consultants, where he serves as a board member and as chairman-elect; a diplomate of the American College of Healthcare Executives, where he serves as a member of the career development committee; a fellow of the Healthcare Financial Management Association; and a member of the American Institute of CPAs and the Georgia Society of CPAs. In 1989 he was named as the recipient of the Chet Minkalis Service Award by the American Association of Healthcare Consultants. *The Health Care Executive's Job Search: Tyler's Guide to Success* is his first book. He is an active tennis player, scuba diver, and sailor, as well as a licensed Coast Guard captain.

Other Books Published by Health Administration Press

▼ ▼ ▼ ▼ ▼ ▼ ▼ ▼ ▼ ▼ ▼ ▼ ▼ ▼ ▼ ▼ ▼ ▼ ▼ ▼

REALLY TRYING: A Career Guide for the Health Services Manager, Second Edition
By Anthony R. Kovner and Alan H. Channing

This popular career guide for health services managers has been revised and updated for students and aspiring managers. Responding to developments in the field and building on the information from the first edition, this version introduces many new topics. Among them are: ethical issues, diversity in the workplace, improved communication with nursing staff, and managing an intensified workload. A comprehensive and readable text, this edition has been expanded to clarify the role and responsibilities of today's managers, to guide their career choices, and ultimately, to enrich their professional lives and enhance the depth of their on-the-job experiences.

REALLY TRYING is divided into three comprehensive parts. The first gives an overview of the management structure in health services human resources management, the second develops skills in human resources management. In part three, the authors present a series of materials from a senior manager's files to illustrate the nature of the challenges health services managers confront daily.

Softbound, 325 pages, 1993, $34.00, Order No. 0935, ISBN 1-56793-001-8 A Health Administration Press Book.

PROTOCOLS FOR HEALTH CARE EXECUTIVE BEHAVIOR: A Factor for Success
By Carson F. Dye

Successful healthcare executives need to understand their own behavior and to know how it affects their relationships with others. This book offers practical guidelines for developing the skills necessary to lead effectively.

Organized in three sections, the book begins with a section on "Managing Yourself: Self-Discipline" and introduces the concept of protocols. Included is a discussion of both general and personal executive protocols, as well as a chapter on executive value systems and tips on building one's professional reputation. The second section sets forth a number of principles for healthcare executives interested in enhancing their relationships with staffs, boards, physicians, and other executives. This section also explores the ethical dimensions of human resource decisions. In the final section the author addresses the particularly significant and timely issues of how to create a gender-neutral workplace and how to embrace cultural diversity.

Hardbound, 231 pages, 1993, $42.00. Order No. 0934, ISBN 1-56793-000-X An American College of Healthcare Executives Management Series Book.

BOOK ORDERING INFORMATION

All Health Administration Press Publications are sent on a 30-day approval. To order call 708/450-9952, fax 708/450-1618, or send your order to: The Foundation of the American College of Healthcare Executives, Publications Service Center, 1951 Cornell Avenue, Melrose Park, IL 60160-1001.